A HISTORY OF CLAIMS
FOR THE SASQUATCH
ON FILM

BIGFOOT'S CAUGHT ON FILM CONTINUE TO
INTRIGUE US, BUT CAN WE LEARN ANYTHING
FROM THESE IMAGES?

MIKE QUAST

UNTOLD PUBLISHING

To report Bigfoot encounters in Minnesota or for further information the author may be contacted at mqstk@aol.com.

Cover design by Doug Hajicek.

INTRODUCTION

Ever since the advent of photography in the mid-to-late 1800s, people have occasionally but consistently been capturing various unexplained phenomena on film. And for almost as long, skeptics have been pointing out how easy it is for the photographic medium to be manipulated to create hoax or "fake" pictures.

Early on, "spirit photographs" taken at seances, cemeteries, and alleged haunted houses the world over caused a sensation. Were these hazy images proof that ghosts walk among us, or just light allowed to leak into the camera? Many were proven fake, while others- including some still being taken today- remain enigmatic.

UFOs, too, have turned up on film time after time, and here again, there is intense debate over the validity of almost every case. Some photos of these mysterious craft show such detail that, if genuine, they are evidence of something truly extraordinary, but again many have turned out to be either hoaxes or mistaken identities of something quite natural.

It's no surprise that the photographic history of cryptozoology- the study of unknown, unproven, unexpected, or out-of-place animals- has followed a similar path. Most of the creatures involved are regarded by their supporters as lying well within the bounds of natural science, not at all "paranormal" or "supernatural," but as our popular culture seems to like to label them as "monsters," it is inevitable that skeptics will rush to try and debunk any apparent evidence of their existence.

The Loch Ness Monster of Scotland is a classic case in point. One of the most photographed of all mysterious creatures, Nessie's image is well known to people around the world. The first grainy black and white surface images began to appear in the early 1930s, and by 1975 dramatic full-color underwater shots had been obtained that showed a clear outline of the animal's long-necked body and diamond-shaped fins, yet Nessie remains officially unrecognized by science. Numerous examples of this scenario involving mystery beasts of land, sea, and air- exist around the globe.

This book, however, focuses on just one such creature- that figure of longstanding legend, the elusive sasquatch (or as it came to be called in northern California in the late 1950s, "Bigfoot," now a household word all across America). Reports of this hairy, apelike forest giant that walks upright like a man go back in white men's history to the time the Vikings landed, and in ancient Native American lore, they have no clear beginning. Though the Pacific Northwest is generally thought of as "Bigfoot Country," areas all over the U.S. and Canada from coast to coast have been involved over the decades. Evidence for the existence of sasquatch in scientific reality includes many thousands of giant footprints up to 18" long or larger, hairs that have been analyzed and found to belong to some unspecific higher primate, and of course, countless numbers of actual sightings by reliable witnesses.

And as everyone with even a casual interest in the subject knows at this point, in October of 1967, two cowboys from Yakima, Washington emerged from the Bluff Creek wilderness of northwest California with color movie film that has gone down in history. This is the famous Patterson film, alleged to be actual footage of a living, breathing sasquatch. But as one can see with a quick check of current zoology texts, this film has not resulted in scientific acceptance for the creature in the over 30 years since its origin, and many skeptics have dismissed it as a hoax without a second look (or even a first in some cases).

The Patterson film is one of the shining stars in the vast array of cryptozoological evidence, having been called "the most famous home movie of all time," and there seems to be an impression in many circles that it is the one and only example of its kind. With so many sightings over the years, people ask, why is this the only film?

The answer, as most serious "Bigfooters" know, is that it is not. Far from it.

I admit to having many personal biases when it comes to the subject of sasquatch, for I believe I saw one myself in the summer of 1976 at age eight. I had no camera handy, nor would it probably have mattered if I had, for the sighting lasted only a few seconds. Still, it had a profound effect on me, and since 1987 I have been involved in seriously investigating sasquatch reports in my home state of Minnesota. Unfortunately, I know of no photographic cases in this particular state, but over the years, I have collected ream upon ream of information on the creatures and their history and have been struck by the number of obscure films and photos that have appeared purporting to show them in the flesh in many diverse places.

The more popular books on the subject have shown around a half dozen vague photographs of what could be sasquatch along with the famous Patterson film, and certain others are available for sale on video. But more than this, a large number of others have been mentioned- usually just brief references- in various books, articles, and newsletters. Sometimes poor reproductions are shown, but more often, they are simply described and left up to our imaginations. The sheer number of these cases seems to have somehow been over-looked even by many serious investigators.

For years I have hoped to see a collection assembled of all these enigmatic images, a book that brought them all together in one place, and early in my years of research, I tried without success to do such a project myself. I found there were many reasons why it was impossible. There were copyright laws involved in some cases. Others involved photos or films that had been described by authors who remembered seeing them years before and knew the stories behind them but had no idea how to reach the owners now. But by far, the most common response to my inquiries was, "The photo you mention is a fake and is useless as evidence." No further comment, end of story.

Now I know I was quite naive in those early inexperienced years, both in fieldwork and in dealing with the politics and personality clashes that are so common between the various factions of sasquatch hunters, but I would like to make one thing perfectly clear:

I have never held any illusions about every single "Bigfoot photo" being genuine.

Without a doubt, and conclusively proven in many cases, several photographic hoaxes have been produced. Being of basic bipedal humanoid shape, the sasquatch lends itself more than any other mysterious creature to such fakery, as a large man in a furry costume can so easily masquerade as one. I have always known this, thus when I was matter-of-factly dismissed with so many assurances that particular pictures were fakes, my attitude was, "Well, I know that... but shouldn't people be allowed to see them anyway?"

Many people in the sasquatch field are concerned with nothing but the hardcore, down-and-dirty physical search for solid proof and will have nothing to do with anything else. Fakery is anathema to these dedicated hunters, and they do have a very good point, as falling for it can harm what little credibility, we might have in our quest to prove the reality of this remarkable animal. Yet even the hoaxes, if viewed in their proper perspective, are a part of sasquatch history, like it or not. For this reason alone- pure anecdotal value- I feel that as many of these photos and films as possible should be made available for all interested parties to study. If known to be fake, they should be labeled as such. If inconclusive, further examination might prove useful. And most important, comparison to the fake (or to mistaken identities such as faraway shots of what turned out to be other animals, inanimate objects, etc.) will always make the genuine article stand out all the more. And how many bona fide filmings of real sasquatches have there been over the years? We may never know for sure, but sheer numbers suggest that there must be at least a few grains of wheat mixed in with the chaff.

This book is not quite the one I still hope to see someday about the sasquatch on film. It is, however, a representation of every visual image I have been able to acquire that has been claimed as evidence of the creature at one time or another. Many more filming cases are presented in written form only where the picture described was unavailable. Every last case involving filming that is personally known to me at this time is included here, though I'm sure there are still more that have eluded me.

These are not the actual photos themselves, however. Rather than wade through the red tape of copyrights and other obstacles to publication, I have employed the use of black and white artist's renderings of each image, a technique I have seen used before with certain Loch Ness photos and been fairly impressed with. In most cases, this technique shows all the detail that would be seen in the original.

I am not a skilled photographer or photo analyst, as I'm sure some will point out, but I have been an artist all my life and have a degree in commercial art. These illustrations are not tracings, but freehand pencil drawings done by placing a grid line pattern over the original photos and copying them square by square. The end product, I feel, is just different enough in minute details to leave my own personal artist's stamp while still remaining true to what was captured by the photographer. Some of the more subtle gray tones do not reproduce well, but I feel that as close a depiction of the originals as possible has been captured.

I have included the opinions of both myself and others about these pictures, but in the end, it is you who must decide- is the photographic medium convincing enough to act as final proof for the existence of sasquatch? Some say yes, while others insist that only a body dead or alive will be acceptable. But either way, I have always had one all-encompassing viewpoint when it comes to photos and films of any unexplained phenomenon, including sasquatch:

In the long run, if they're not good enough to act as the final proof... does it really matter if they're real or fake?

1

THE PATTERSON FILM

The case at hand here is literally the most famous sasquatch story of all time, and there is virtually nothing that can be said about it that will not already be intimately familiar to practically anyone with an interest in the field, but to exclude it from a book on sasquatch filmings for that reason would be an intolerable crime. Thus, Mr. Roger Clarence Patterson...

He is legendary to modem sasquatch hunters, and his film is spoken of by many in reverent tones as if it was some holy relic or the cure to some dread illness (only a few in the field have doubted its authenticity). One must wonder what Patterson himself would think of all this attention had he not succumbed to Hodgkin's Disease at age 38, just over four scant years after the event that defined his life. He was a jack of all trades from Yakima, Washington- rodeo cowboy, boxer, inventor, promoter, health food nut, avid outdoorsman, and family man- who entered the hunt for sasquatch when a 1959 article on California's "Bigfoot" by Ivan T. Sanderson in True magazine captivated him. He searched throughout the Pacific Northwest, most notably in the pre-eruption landscape of Mount St. Helens, Washington and in the Bluff Creek area of Del Norte County, California, the birthplace of Bigfoot, and found enough compelling evidence to keep him going over several years in spite of poor finances and the lack of focus some say he sometimes suffered from. He probably had no more skill or expertise than others in the field he associated with within those days (John Green, Rene Dahinden, etc.), but is rather regarded as the one who got lucky. And then some.

Even schoolchildren interested in Bigfoot know the date by heart at this point- October 20, 1967. The previous year Patterson had published a book, "Do Abominable Snowmen of America Really Exist?", illustrated with his own talented drawings, and now with limited funds had come once again to Bluff Creek in response to word that new Bigfoot tracks had recently been seen, working on a documentary film. With him was his friend Bob Gimlin, also of Yakima, who wasn't even sure he believed in the creature but agreed to come along for the chance to train his horses in rugged terrain. The two were camped in the Bluff Creek wilderness, shooting scenes of the landscape and hoping to find fresh tracks, and it was Gimlin's idea to check the banks of the creek itself on that fateful Friday afternoon; Patterson had had another area in mind. At around 1:20 p.m., with both men on horseback and leading a third horse to carry supplies, they rode around a large mass of logs (pushed up by spring floods) and into history.

The first thing that happened was that the horses panicked and reared, and Patterson's fell over onto its side, crushing a stirrup with his foot still in it. At some point during those confused seconds, the men caught sight of the cause of the commotion: a large hairy creature crouched on the opposite bank which immediately stood and began to walk away on two legs, not hurrying but never pausing.

Neither man had ever seen a sasquatch before (though Patterson may have heard the vocalizations of one at least once), yet considering the circumstances, both reacted remarkably well. Gimlin steadied his horse while Patterson managed to pull the 16-mm Cine-Kodak movie camera from his saddlebag and, despite his injured foot, ran toward the retreating creature, filming as he went and shouting for Gimlin to cover him. As Patterson's horse and the pack animal ran off, Gimlin rode across the creek with his

30.06 rifle at the ready in case the creature attacked, pointing the weapon in its direction but not actually aiming. He would recall later that if he'd had a rope, he probably could have gotten close enough to lasso it (and what a film that would have made!).

Patterson had gotten to within about 80 feet of the creature when it swung around and shot him a glance that made him stop. Later he would describe its attitude as like "when the umpire tells you 'One more word and you're out of the game!'" but he continued to film from a stationary position as it continued on away from him, finally disappearing into the dense forest, at which point the film ran out. He had captured over 23 feet of color footage (952 frames) of the first and only sasquatch he ever saw in his life.

The men decided not to follow the creature. Though their recollections of certain details would vary later, both agreed that its large breasts indicated it was a female, and they feared it might have a mate nearby. Instead, they reloaded the camera and shot footage of the clear 14 ½" footprints it had left on the sandy creek bank (footage which was subsequently lost somehow, though excerpts from it have turned up in various places) and made plaster casts of both left and right prints. After rounding up the horses, they then drove out to civilization (possibly the town of Eureka, possibly Arcata- accounts vary) to mail the film to Patterson's brother-in-law Al de Atley, and placed a call to the British Columbia Museum to inquire as to the possibility of someone bringing in tracking dogs to pick up the creature's trail. The museum in fam contacted investigator John Green, who tried in vain to arrange for some scientist to travel to the site before too much time had passed.

But Mother Nature had her own agenda. Nightfall found Patterson and Gimlin back at their camp, but a sudden rainstorm and flash flood threatened to wash out the road, and they had to make a perilous retreat out of the woods.

One adventure was over, but one of a different kind was just beginning- that of presenting the film to the public and to science. Patterson was anxious to show it to the world, sure he had the proof that had been sought for so long. Al de Atley was the first person to see the film that millions have now seen. Soon after, Patterson and investigators John Green, Rene Dahinden, and Jim McClarin viewed it for the first time at De Atley's home in Yakima. And just what did they see?

In the original, the creature is not even as large as the sprocket holes in the film, resulting in a rather anti-climactic effect. In the book "Sasquatch Apparitions" by the late Barbara Wasson, Bob Gimlin stated, "Of course I thought the film should have been a lot better than that. I thought the film would be very good. I thought you could be able to just pick the flies off its nose, that close." Subsequent enlargements, however, brought out the images we all know so well today- not as sharp and clear as a professional wildlife film, perhaps, but still striking in their detail.

The first seconds are just a furious blur of bouncing motion as Patterson runs and jumps over rough terrain and crosses the creek while filming. He then steadies himself, probably crouching, and we see the creature walking (not running) purposefully from left to right against the autumn forest backdrop, swinging its arms in a smooth, bent-kneed stride unlike the bouncy, straight-legged walk of a human being. It is covered with black hair except in small patches such as the face, where grayish skin shows through. The body is massive, proportioned like that of a man but much broader and with muscles that Gimlin compared to those of the horses he had spent his life observing. Large, pendulous, hair-covered breast ("mammary glands" as Gimlin has called them, another animal reference) seem to identify the creature as female, but its head is peaked at the top like that of a male gorilla. Enlargements of the face show a heavy brow ridge, deep-set eyes, a wide nose, and no visible ears. The neck is very short, almost non-existent, and when the creature turns toward the camera in what Patterson thought was a gesture of warning, it turns its entire upper body rather than just the head, for just as with a gorilla, the neck is too short for the chin to pass over the shoulder. This results in the most famous of all the images from the film, frame #352, reproduced countless times on book covers and in at least half the magazine and newspaper articles ever written on sasquatch- arms wide apart, right leg forward, left leg mostly hidden behind a log, and face directly toward the camera. From this point, the creature continues on and turns away from the creek bank, gradually disappearing into the forest. During these final moments, the broad back is displayed, and one gets the best sense of how far below the shoulders the head is actually set. Here also are the only views of the feet, with hairless soles and five toes briefly but clearly seen. There is no clear distinction of the other digits, apparently obscured by hair, but the bending of the hand does suggest fingers.

As shown elsewhere in this book, there had been a few photographs taken in previous years that purported to show sasquatches, but none of these were very widely known. Patterson's film was definitely the first of its quality and in its potential to sway scientific interest, but John Green and others cautioned him that it would be better for his credibility if he let authorities come to him rather than running all over the country shouting "Look at this!" But Patterson's enthusiasm proved stronger than his patience. The first showing for scientists was at the University of British Columbia, where the film caused quite a stir but failed to create the sensation that was hoped for. Showings in other cities raised even less interest, and though Life magazine showed some interest, it quickly dwindled when the American Museum of Natural History assured the editors the film was most definitely a fake after one brief run-through.

There was no in-depth scientific analysis of the film, nor did the scientists even seem to think one necessary. Such creatures did not exist, after all, so why waste time on a film that had to be a hoax? Only primatologist John Napier of the Smithsonian Institute (later author of a popular book on the Bigfoot phenomenon to be referred to shortly) and biologist and paranormal researcher Ivan T. Sanderson (Patterson's original inspiration) paid any serious attention.

It was in the February 1968 issue of Argosy, a popular mens' adventure magazine, rather than the more prestigious Life that frames from the film were first presented to the public, with an article by Sanderson entitled "First Photos of 'Bigfoot,' California's 'Abominable Snowman.'"

The first amateur investigation at the film site, meanwhile, had been done about nine or ten days after the filming by Bob Titmus, a veteran of the search for Bigfoot in northern California since the late 1950s (now deceased) who brought his skills as a taxidermist and animal tracker to bear in examining the film creature's 14 1/2" tracks (which had actually first been seen the day after the filming by forester Lyle Laverty, who did little more than photograph them). Titmus made plaster casts of a series of consecutive prints, then followed the trail and was able to determine that the creature had bank.

The Patterson film creature striding in profile along the of Bluff Creek.

Sat down in some ferns in a spot 80 or 90 feet above the creek and 125 to 150 yards from where Patterson and Gimlin had excitedly reorganized themselves, perhaps watching them. From the depth of the tracks, Titmus estimated that the creature must have weighed 600 to 700 pounds.

Further insight was made at the film site in June of 1968 by John Green. His idea was to make a comparison film with a large man walking in about the same place where the creature had walked so as to determine its exact physical dimensions. The model used was fellow investigator Jim McClarin, a student at Humboldt State University in Arcata who stood 6' 5", just a shade under the height that most serious studies of the film have arrived at for the creature. Green's conclusions established a height of 6' 8", shoulders 34" across, a neck width of 12", and similar massive proportions overall.

Since then, of course, the Patterson Bigfoot film has been the subject of intense debate and publicity. No one in that time has been more associated with it than Rene Dahinden, who owns the current rights to it and has spent much time and energy in court fighting over its various legal entanglements. It was also he who went to the most effort to have competent experts finally take a hard-eyed look at the footage, and when American scientists turned a blind eye, he went elsewhere. In 1971 Dahinden took the film both to England and to the former Soviet Union. (Perhaps the most significant response in America at that point had been from Walt Disney Studios, who in 1969 told John Green that they would not have been able to duplicate the film with existing technology of the time.)

Frame #352- The money shot. The single most famous image of Bigfoot ever, reproduced countless times the world over.

Dr. D.W. Grieve, an expert on biomechanics at the Royal Free Hospital School of Medicine in London, did one of the first well-known studies of the film, and at this point, it began to be a major point of argument that Patterson could not recall the exact film speed he had had the camera set for. (He had been filming the Bluff Creek scenery at 24 fps, which was best suited for television, but wasn't sure if he had changed the setting prior to encountering the sasquatch.) After carefully weighing the possibility that the film showed a human being in a costume based on the creature's proportions and gait, Dr. Grieve concluded:

"My subjective impressions have oscillated between total acceptance of the Sasquatch on the grounds that the film would be difficult to fake, to one of irrational rejection based on an emotional response to the possibility that the Sasquatch actually exists ... The possibility of a very clever fake cannot be ruled out on the evidence of the film. A man could have sufficient height and suitable proportions to mimic the longitudinal dimensions of the Sasquatch. The shoulder breadth, however, would be difficult to achieve without giving an unnatural appearance to the arm swing and shoulder contours. The possibility of fakery is ruled out if the speed of the film was 16 or 18 fps. In these conditions, a normal human being could not duplicate the observed pattern, which would suggest that the Sasquatch must possess a very different locomotor system to that of man."

The analysis by the Russians was even more thorough and delivered probably the strongest support for the film's validity to date. Their country had its own manlike creature reported to exist in its mountainous wilderness areas, known by such names as *Almista* and *Kaptar,* or sometimes as "Snowman" in comparison to the more famous abominable denizen of the Himalayas, and investigators there were beginning to communicate with those in America for insight into the nature and possible relation of their respective creatures. After numerous showings of Patterson's film by Dahinden in Moscow, researchers Dmitri Bayanov and Igor Bourtsev, as well as biomechanics expert Dr. Dmitri Donskoy of the U.S.S.R. Central Institute of Physical Culture, subjected it to an in-depth analysis in which they concluded that it was unquestionably genuine. Their points of argument are very complex, detailed in full in Bayanov's recent book "America's Bigfoot: Fact, Not Fiction," but one of the most valuable of their findings was Bourtsev's conclusion on the film speed. By concentrating on the bouncing in the first moments of the footage, which he reasoned had to correspond with the steps taken by Patterson, he found that if the setting had been 24 fps, then Patterson had been taking six steps per second, which would mean that a man with an injured foot wearing cowboy boots had run faster than a world-class sprinter over rough terrain. A confident conclusion of 16 fps was made, which according to Dr. Grieve, would mean that "the possibility of fakery is ruled out."

Less decisive conclusions were reached by the Smithsonian's Dr. John Napier in his 1972 book "Bigfoot: The Yeti and Sasquatch in Myth and Reality." In this book, Napier concluded that the sasquatch most probably did exist, yet his thoughts on the Patterson film seemed to waffle curiously back and forth for a study that was supposed to bring scientific scrutiny to the subject. He was of the opinion that the creature's walk was generally consistent with that of a human being, and that its various physical features seemed to combine both male and female primate physiology, a fact that has been noted by other skeptics over the years. The large breasts, for instance, are obviously a female trait, yet the bony crest atop the head is a characteristic of male gorillas and orangutans. Napier also stated:

"The presence of buttocks, a human hallmark, is at total variance with the ape-like nature of the superstructure ... The upper half of the body bears some resemblance to an ape, and the lower half is typically human. It is almost impossible to conceive that such structural hybrids could exist in nature."

Yet after these skeptical comments, he rounded out his section on the film by

stating:

"...there was nothing in the film which would prove conclusively that this was a hoax. In effect, what I meant was that I could not see the zipper, and I still can't... There I think we must leave the matter. Perhaps it was a man dressed up in a monkey-skin; if so, it was a brilliantly executed hoax, and the unknown perpetrator will take his place with the great hoaxers of the world. Perhaps it was the first film of a new type of hominid, quite unknown to science... "

All in all, it was a lack of commitment either way.

Napier was English. It has often been said that no serious scientific study of the film has ever been done in America, but this is not really true. Physical anthropologist

Dr. Grover Krantz, formerly of Washington State University in Pullman (now retired), one of the celebrities of the sasquatch field and one of the few scientists willing to publicly state his belief in the creature, has studied the film closely and commented on his conclusions both in the early 1970s and more recently in his 1992 book "Big Footprints: A Scientific Inquiry into the Reality of Sasquatch." Krantz has his opponents in the field, however (largely due to his endorsement of dubious evidence from Washington's Blue Mountains detailed later in this book), including Rene Dahinden, and it appears that the American study being called for is any besides his. Nevertheless, in addition to pointing out how the creature's feet raised small mounds of dirt in the middle of its tracks as it stepped- something a rigid, inflexible fake foot could not do- he has convincingly addressed many of the arguments put forth by skeptics of the film:

1. The creature has female breasts, yet shows a male crest on its head- Krantz has correctly pointed out that the "sagittal crest" on the heads of male gorillas and orangutans is not really related to gender, but to size. Its purpose is to anchor the massive jaws of these animals, and it so happens that only males of these species grow big enough to require it. But if a female primate grew to the size of the Patterson film creature, it would very likely have such a crest as well.

2. The creature's breasts appear to be hair-covered, whereas the breasts of known primates are generally hairless- Early on, Krantz responded to this rather sarcastically with, "I don't know what the breast of a sasquatch *ought* to look like," and added that the bulge on the creature's chest might not actually be breasts but the laryngeal air sacs that inflate to great size in the throat and chest area in some great apes, particularly the orangutan. But in his book, he qualified this with, "Actually I do not find this to be as likely an explanation as that they are breasts." It is simply a matter of not making broad generalizations about what traits a totally brand-new species ought to have.

3. The bottoms of the creature's feet are unusually light in color- This is common, Krantz notes, even in dark-skinned Africans whose soles simply contain less pigment than other parts of the body. (It is also worth noting that the creature was standing in shallow water when first encountered, and that its necessarily wet feet in the film are the exact same gray as the sand it is walking on.)

4. The creature's walk appears human-like and is therefore likely to be that of a large man in a costume- Krantz concedes that indeed the walk is somewhat human-like, which is exactly what we should expect for any bipedal primate. But as pointed out by other studies, the walk does show marked differences from that of man, and Krantz

makes his most important arguments against the man-in-a-costume theory by simply noting the proportions of the creature's body. With the width of the shoulders and chest, it is simply mathematically impossible for any man alive- no matter how large- to fit into such a costume and still demonstrate the freedom of movement and apparent musculature that is shown in the film. The differences may be subtle, but there is just no way around them.

The findings of professional scientists like Grieve, Donskoy, Krantz, and others seem to lend considerable weight to the potential validity of the Patterson film, but support has also come from more controversial sources- some, in fact, that the top names in the sasquatch field would much rather do without. For instance, Jon Eric Beckjord- an

investigator of various paranormal phenomena who has operated a cryptozoology museum and supports a supernatural-type origin for sasquatch- put forth one very unusual theory. What appears to be the creature's breasts in the film, he says, is actually an infant creature clinging to its mother's chest. Almost all serious supporters of the film have denounced this idea with barely a second thought, and even Bob Gimlin emphatically stated that there was no way he and Patterson would have failed to notice something so significant. It seems to be a matter of peculiar illusions in a few individual frames of the film that gave birth to this view. (I myself see exactly what Beckjord seems to be talking about, but if he is right, his "infant" would have no legs, and I feel this theory can safely be discarded.) Further wild claims were made by Beckjord in 2000 when he attempted to sell a copy of the film on the Internet, falsely claiming to have the legal right to do so (and for $1 million!) and stated that he had located a metal tube on the creature's arm suggesting that it may have been "a genetic experiment gone wild, or else an alien." Enough said.

No proof of a hoax has ever been successfully put forth, though some have tried. The 1990s, in fact, fumed out to be a big decade for such attempts. Ray Wallace, a notorious figure from the early days of Bigfoot in the Pacific Northwest who is featured prominently in a later chapter of this book, told naturalist/author Robert Michael Pyle,

"I know exactly which Yakima Indian was in that monkey suit," in Pyle's 1995 book "Where Bigfoot Walks: Crossing the Dark Divide." Meanwhile, investigator Cliff Crook of Bigfoot Central in Bothell, Washington, offers a booklet entitled "The Abominable Snowjob" to explain why he feels the film must be fake (mainly anatomical points already explained by Grover Krantz).

Crook teamed with another Bigfoot buff, Chris Murphy, to denounce the film by announcing in the Associated Press on January 9, 1999, that a close examination of certain frames had revealed some type of latch resembling a wine bottle opener low on the creature's torso. Investigator Daniel Perez responded to the charge that same month in his Bigfoot Times newsletter, suggesting certain personality-related reasons why Crook and Murphy would become detractors of the film and adding, "What Chris Murphy claims to see in 'enhanced' frames from Patterson's film, a wine-bottle opener or an ornate latch, was not noted by a recent forensic examination of the film by Jeff Glickman." (The study he refers to was an attempt to bring out sharper detail by digitizing the film, carried out by the North American Science Institute in association with the former Bigfoot Research Project headed by investigator Peter Byrne.)

Both Cliff Crook and Ray Wallace, it should be noted, have promoted other films and photos alleged to show genuine sasquatches.

One serious attempt at writing off the Patterson film as a hoax came in 1997 when movie director John Landis said in an interview with journalist Scott Essman, "That famous piece of film of Bigfoot walking in the woods that was touted as the real thing was just a suit made by John Chambers." Landis had worked with Chambers on the highly successful film "Planet of the Apes," which used realistic makeup- not full-body suits- to turn actors into apemen.

The accusation was backed up by Howard Berger of Hollywood's KNB Effects Group. "It was like a gag to be played on the guy who shot it. The guy never knew it was a hoax his friends played on him."

Mike McCracken Jr., a makeup artist who worked with Chambers, stated, "I'd say with absolute certainty that John was responsible. A gorilla suit expert, Bob Burns, said that the alleged Bigfoot shows evidence of a water bag in the stomach area- a trick used to make a gorilla suit move like real flesh." (A "trick," however, never even suggested by the several scientific skeptics who have denounced the film in any number of other ways over the years.)

In May of 1996, CNI News had reported, "Harry Kemball, director and screenwriter at golden Eagle Productions, told 'X' CHRONICLES researchers that he was at the Canwest 16mm film editing room in 1967 when Roger Patterson and his friends put together his Bigfoot hoax on 16mm film ... According to Kemball, they all laughed and joked about the rental of the gorilla costume and the construction of the big feet."

But here is where the "Hollywood Hoax" theory seems to lose its strength. Either Patterson faked the film himself, or "the guy never knew it was a hoax his friends played on him." It cannot be both ways, after all. (And even many skeptics admit that if the film is a fake, the costume is an ingenious creation, absolutely not a commonly rented gorilla suit.)

The most serious and concentrated attempt to write off the Patterson film, however, came on December 28, 1998, when FOX t.v. aired a special entitled "World's Greatest Hoaxes- Secrets Finally Revealed," which presented alleged films of a variety of paranormal-type events and proceeded to tear them apart. The show was hosted by actor Lance Henriksen, star of the popular series "Millennium," and as I am a fan of his, I could only hope that he was unaware of the true nature of some of what he was paid to say.

Admittedly, most of what was shown on the program actually was fake. A completely ridiculous film of a tyrannosaurus rex lumbering around in a park in the middle of London, for instance- although apparently some people actually fell for it. Other items- such as the notorious "Alien Autopsy," the UFO films of Billy Meier, and certain Loch Ness monster photos- will probably be debated and remain inconclusive in the minds of many for years to come. When it came to Bigfoot, three films were presented. A video from Ohio and another purporting to show a Himalayan yeti both suffered from their subjects staying around far too long to have their pictures taken, as well as foliage in the yeti film that looked curiously American rather than Asian. But then there was the Patterson film...

FOX began by presenting Kai K. Korff, known from the field of UFO study rather than that of cryptozoology. He contended that Patterson's film was most definitely a fake, and as evidence pointed out such things as a line of dark fur running down the creature's back (implication- zipper) and how the bottom of a foot seen in one frame did not match the tracks, Patterson and Gimlin said the creature made.

From there, the show moved into a much more serious allegation. Clyde o. Reinke, a rancher, and businessman who was once a manager for a film company called American National Enterprises in Salt Lake City, stated categorically that Roger

Patterson was permanently employed by them as a cameraman, and that he was assigned to go out and create a Bigfoot film to be used as an attraction that would draw bigger audiences to the company's nature films. American National did produce a film called "Big Foot: Man or Beast" that used the Patterson film, but though Reinke said Patterson's status with the company had always been a closely guarded secret, he produced no documentation to back this up. In other words, there was no paper trail to be found.

Reinke also alleged that one Mr. Jerry Romney, a very large man who is now an insurance agent, was the man in the Bigfoot costume, but Romney also appeared on the show and flatly denied this. His walk was compared to that of the creature and very unconvincingly insinuated to be similar.

Some of it will be repetitive, but I'd like to share parts of an open letter to FOX that I sent them in response to the show. It also appeared in the February 1999 issue of the Bigfoot Co-Op. and I think it sums up the entire case quite well:

"This is in response to your recent program "WORLD'S GREATEST HOAXES...

"...my reason for this letter is your treatment of the 1967 Roger Patterson 'Bigfoot' film. I have been involved in investigating reports of a sasquatch (the term I prefer) for many years and treat the subject with great seriousness.

"The other two 'Bigfoot'-type films you showed- one of an American Midwest area creature and one supposedly of an Asian yeti- are indeed fakes, as are most such films that come in anonymously. But the Patterson film is far from anonymous. Full disclosure of who (and what) Patterson was and of every detail of the filming is a matter of public record. His film is not a fake, and I wish to present several points to indicate this, for your presentation made it clear that you relied solely on the sources presented for your information and did not take the time to talk to the many qualified people who have worked at analyzing the film over the past 30 years, some of whom knew Patterson personally.

"Within the program, itself were three relevant points:

"1. The man named as the one inside the alleged 'creature costume' is not elusive but freely consented to your interview and denied the charge. It is one man's word against another, thus canceling each other out.

"(And when the man's walk was compared to the creature's and said to be clearly similar, that was nonsense. Why, just because he is tall and heavyset? The man showed a straight-legged bouncy walk as do all humans, while the film creature walks with a bent-knee stride that has been remarked upon by various scientists as being quite unhuman.)

"2. You pointed out how various points on the creature's body just 'look fake,' such as the dark stripe on its back, suggested as being a zipper. Such observations can be made only by qualified zoologists, and even then, no one can really say what traits a totally unclassified animal should have just because other similar types do. The dark strip may very well be just a peculiar shadow effect along the spine anyway.

"(And in fact, in the 1972 book 'BIGFOOT: THE YETI AND SASQUATCH IN MYTH AND REALITY' primatologist John Napier of no less than the Smithsonian Institution commented on his analysis of the film and specifically stated that he 'could not find the zipper.')

"Also, your analyst pointed to a frame showing the creature's left foot and said it could not have made the footprints associated with the film. However, a frame just before this shows a much clearer outline of the creature's right foot, and it matches the prints exactly. Clearly, the left foot is simply captured at an odd angle that distorts it.

"3. In your comments on the other two films, you rightly pointed out the obvious human-like behavior of the alleged creatures, how they stuck around to be filmed rather than fleeing like a real wild creature. The Patterson film creature does the exact opposite of this, fleeing from human contact and not reappearing- a fact you did not dwell on.

"On now to a number of documented facts on Patterson himself and his film that contradict any claim of a hoax:

"1. By all accounts of many people who knew him- many of whom do not know each other- Patterson was a poor man, a jack of all trades and master of none who was almost always in debt.

"2. The camera Patterson used to film the creature- a Cine-Kodak K-100 16mm home movie camera- was rented and not even paid for, a fact that subsequently led to a warrant being issued for his arrest.

"3. Patterson had investigated sasquatch reports and searched for the creature for six years prior to the filming without any major break-throughs, had published an obscure book in 1966 ('DO ABOMINABLE SNOWMEN OF AMERICA REALLY EXIST?') to try and raise funds, and was well known to other investigators in the sasquatch field. In 1967, he was working on a documentary film of his own- publicly, not in secret- and was in the Bluff Creek, California area at the time of the filming in response to a call from storekeeper Al Hodgson of nearby Willow Creek, alerting him to fresh footprints recently found in the area.

"(Points 1-3 alone effectively rule out the idea put forth in your program that Patterson was secretly a full-time employee of a professional film company hired to go out and create a Bigfoot film to increase ticket sales at their nature movies. Strange, isn't it, that

Patterson- who was dying of Hodgkin's disease at the time- remained penniless after the filming? And would the company not have supplied him with a more professional model camera? Finally, Hodgson's call indicates Patterson's spur-of-the-moment trip to Bluff Creek- it was not planned out in-depth.)

"4. After the filming, on the same day (10/20/67), Patterson is documented as having done the following:

"A. He mailed the film to his brother-in-law Al de Atley for processing, not to some professional studio.

"B. Next, he called the British Columbia Museum to inquire as to the possibility of having tracking dogs brought to the site to pick up the creature's trail. This did not materialize, but he could not have known that it would not.

"Neither of these acts would be expected from a hoaxer- especially the dogs- unless he wanted to be promptly exposed.

"5. There were at least three forest roads in the general vicinity of the film site down which unexpected travelers might have come at any time- an unlikely spot in which to stage a hoax. (And incidentally, it is not just a claimed site- landmarks in the film easily identified it as the spot Patterson said it was, and it has been thoroughly studied by other investigators.

As the creature disappeared into the forest, Patterson managed to capture a few images of its feet which matched the 14-1/2" tracks it left behind. This frame also gives a good impression of the shoulder width and the shortness of the neck.

"6. Finally, you totally ignored one of the most important factors of all. While rightly stating that Patterson is no longer living and able to be questioned, you did not even mention the existence of the man who was with him that day, Bob Gimlin, who still resides in Yakima, Washington. Gimlin has always maintained that they encountered a real sasquatch at Bluff Creek, has never profited from the film at all, and has been offered large sums of money to 'come clean' about the alleged hoax. His answer: 'I'm already telling the truth.'

"Your exclusion of Gimlin is all the more odd in that you have interviewed him before for the series 'Sightings' a few years back. One would think you could have at least used that footage to offer balanced opinions when making such serious allegations about the film.

"(It could be claimed that Gimlin was actually the first victim of Patterson's hoax, but this too is discounted by several points. Patterson and Gimlin camped together for several days, making any communications between Patterson and his costumed accomplice very difficult to accomplish in secret, not to mention the fact that Gimlin could have seen the vehicle necessary to bring the costume into the area. Plus, it was Gimlin's idea to explore that particular stream bank on that afternoon, so how could Costume-man have known where they would be and place himself accordingly? Finally, Gimlin states that Patterson yelled 'Cover me!' as he ran toward the creature with his camera, as Gimlin was holding a loaded rifle, and in the excitement of the moment, there was no guarantee that he would not shoot. Costume-man would have been foolish indeed to risk his life in such a manner, not to mention the risk of being caught and unmasked since both men were riding horses.)

"Now, I would like to present some of the actual scientific analyses that have been done to vindicate the Patterson film. Despite what seems to be the popular misconception, most scientists who have labeled it a hoax have never actually done an in-depth study of it but have based their conclusions on preconceived notions that the sasquatch could not possibly exist; therefore, the film must be a fake. However ..."

The letter then went through the findings of Grieve, the Russians, Krantz, and Titmus, adding a few personal comments. Where Grieve had stated, "In these conditions (16 or 18 fps film speed) a normal human being could not duplicate the observed pattern ..." I added that in this context, a large man nearly seven feet tall as shown on the FOX program still qualified as a "normal human being." I also added that the film was once studied by experts in the design of prosthetic limbs who found nothing unnatural in the creature's movements. In mentioning how Titmus had followed the creature's trail from the film site and found where it had sat down in the foliage, I pointed out that "Patterson never even hinted at there being any such traces as he would have if they were there but of his own design." Finally, after quoting Gimlin from an earlier episode of FOX's show "Sightings" on how natural the creature's muscles had appeared to move

underneath the hair, I suggested that perhaps the FOX people should go back and examine their own archives.

I concluded the letter:

"I wanted to provide FOX with this information in the hopes that if your program is run again, you will provide updates and more balanced information. There have been a number of other such hoax claims made against the Patterson film in the past couple of years-some of which are completely different and contradict each other-but they do not and can not contradict the scientific facts that have been established. It is a peculiar thing that extraordinary claims are always picked apart in minute detail to prove that they could not be, but the second the claim of 'Hoax!' is made, it is accepted without a second thought. Must not both sides of the argument be studied with equal precision? The trouble in the sasquatch field is that the true facts are readily available only in obscure newsletters and the occasional book that reaches only a tiny percent of the population- but everyone watches t.v. That is why you should filly research every side of any story. As one of your own most popular programs so eloquently puts it, 'The truth is out there.'"

The sudden intense barrage of hoax claims in the 1990s was really quite odd, and one must wonder why it was suddenly so important to so many diverse people to try and prove the film a fraud. Could there have been a connection between them all? It doesn't really matter, for whether there was or not, their several completely different hoax stories cancel each other out quite effectively.

The story has been told- beginning, middle, and end. The evidence is in, and it has failed to provide absolute, incontrovertible proof for the existence of sasquatch. The Patterson film has been subjected to extensive scientific study, and no proof of a hoax has been found, yet most scientists still refuse to accept it. No, it will take another story to do that, whether it involves another film or something more tangible.

But I, like most in the sasquatch field, believe the film does indeed show a real live North American primate species that has yet to be classified by science. No other film or photo has approached its quality or stood up to so much scrutiny without being officially dismissed or set aside as inconsequential. Of course, there are skeptics; there always are. Of course, there are those who claim to know every detail of how the hoax was staged- there are also those who claim to know every detail of how Elvis faked his death, or who know the exact date and time of the second coming of Christ.

It has been over three decades. The average lifespan of the great apes is around 40 years. Thus if the sasquatch follows the same rule, the subject of Patterson's film- seemingly a mature adult at the time- is most likely no longer living. But perhaps the subject of the next great film- the one that goes even farther toward proof, perhaps?- is in its healthy prime and roaming some unknown American forest even now.

2

THE BEASTLY GALLERY

Welcome now to a most unique gallery of photographic art, a display as diverse as it is compelling. There are no classic masterpieces hanging on these walls, nothing approaching the level of even the least known professional wildlife photographers, yet who among us can resist a look? For the possibility of scientific evidence for the existence of a truly remarkable creature lies here in the Beastly Gallery. Not proof, perhaps, but evidence at the very least.

That is, if any of these photos and films are genuine. Are they?

What is certain is this: If the sasquatch does not exist, then everything here is either a hoax or a mistake. But even if it does, there are still certainly hoaxes and mistakes in this collection, mixed in just possibly- with a few rare and precious images of real, living crypto-zoological primates popularly known as Bigfoot or sasquatch.

In some of these cases, fairly sound identifications have been made. Others remain open to interpretation, and the word "inconclusive" will often appear in the evaluations given here. These evaluations are my own, and readers are free to make their own judgments.

My categories of evaluation are as follows:

TENTATIVE ACCEPTANCE: Most likely a sasquatch.

COMMON ANIMAL: A known animal misidentified as sasquatch.
NATURAL FORMATION: An inanimate object misidentified as a sasquatch.
HOAX: Deliberate fakery; an inanimate object or costumed human portraying sasquatch.
INCONCLUSIVE: Not of good enough quality and/or not enough information to make a firm evaluation.

A sixth category would be "DEFINITIVE EVIDENCE," but I feel the 1967 Patterson film already discussed is the only example so far worthy of such a label.

PHOTOGRAPHER: Unknown
LOCATION: Near Lilooet, British Columbia
DATE: Early 20th Century
APPEARS IN- "The Evidence for Bigfoot and Other Man-Beasts" by Janet & Colin Bord

Very little is known about this photo except that it shows an unidentified animal supposedly shot by some trappers.

The subject of the picture is lying dead, stretched out in the snow with a pair of snowshoes near its head to give scale. It appears slender and quite long in the body, with a rope or cord tied around its forelimbs. The head is small and roundish. Some detail in the face- light patches in the otherwise dark hair- is evident but very vague.

One impression given is that if this is a sasquatch, it would have to be a young one, owing to its lack of bulk. In turning the picture to get a vertical perspective, what

would be the hip area seems somewhat low for this to be an upright-walking creature. Identification would be easier if the entire animal was visible, but its lower legs are out of frame, at least in the published version.

Veteran sasquatch investigator John Green of British Columbia, however, states that he has identified it and that it is some species of cat (probably a mountain lion). In a letter to the author, he wrote:

"As to the Lilooet photo, there is no story to go with it, that's the whole problem, but I have studied the actual photograph with a magnifying glass, and there is no doubt the thing is a cat. The face is not buried in the snow; it is lying on its side... Quite obviously, it has no shoulders, and those things on the ends of its front legs are paws, not hands. I don't have the photo now, and I don't remember how it ever got mixed up with the sasquatch question, but of course, it shouldn't be."

When viewed in this light, what some might take for a small tuft of hair on top of the creature's head easily becomes a cat's pointed ear. Green's explanation seems to be the most likely one.

CONCLUSION: Common animal.

PHOTOGRAPHER: Name unknown
LOCATION: Alaska
DATE: 1948 (Unpublished)

Pennsylvania sasquatch researcher Joan Jeffers (now deceased) supplied this shot, one frame of a very brief sequence of 8mm cine film taken by her uncle decades earlier. Her accompanying letter stated:

"The film my uncle took in Alaska in the late 1940s is intriguing. It certainly looks like a very large, hairy biped walking through a field at a great distance. The segment is just over two seconds long, so it is difficult to make out much ... I had some home movies put on video-tape last year, or I might never have seen this. (The print she sent was a photo of a t.v. screen showing the video.) My father's family were lumberjacks in Pennsylvania and New York... I have been interested in the "old man" since 1938 when I was six and overheard tales of the creature. I recalled my uncle saying he had seen one in Alaska and took pictures, but never saw the film until now."

California investigator Daniel Perez mentioned the film in the March 2000 issue of his Bigfoot Times newsletter. Perez wrote:

"The film was shot while Joan's uncle was driving his truck along a road ... I called Joan Jeffers on June 10th, 1994, at which time she told me the film was shot with large electrical towers nearby and that her aunt saw it, too... The filmed subject was walking through a field of dried grass, according to Ms. Jeffers, and the camera was rolling before the subject came into view."

An animal killed by trappers near Lilooet, British Columbia, in the early 20th century, mysterious-looking in the picture but identified as probably a cougar.

A frame from the film shot by Joan Jeffers' uncle in Alaska in 1948.

The print supplied to me actually shows very little, just a tiny dark vertical form at extreme range in dazzling bright green surroundings- tall grass in the foreground and trees behind. It could just as easily be a stump as a living creature. Apparently, the moving film is somewhat more impressive, but at only two seconds could not be considerably so.

(One curious detail: Color film was not in wide use in the 1940s.)

CONCLUSION: Inconclusive.

PHOTOGRAPHER: Zack Hamilton
LOCATION: Three Sisters Wilderness, Oregon
DATE: 1960
APPEARS IN- "Do Abominable Snowmen of America Really Exist?" by Roger Patterson; "On the Track of the Sasquatch" by John Green; "The Search for Big FootMonster, Myth or Man?" by Peter Byrne; "The Mysterious Monsters" by Robert & Frances Guenette; "America's Bigfoot: Fact, Not Fiction" by Dmitri Bayanov; San Francisco Chronicle, December 14th, 1965; The Track Record #32, October 1993; "Ancient Mysteries: Bigfoot" (A & E t.v.)

In 1960 Zack Hamilton- described as the typical "grizzled woodsman"- brought in a roll of film for development at a San Francisco camera shop. He claimed that a hairy two-legged creature had stalked him on a recent excursion in the Three Sisters Wilderness of central Oregon and that he had it on film. He never came back to pick up the photos, but true to his word, they seemed to show what he had described. The shop's assistant manager said he got "prickly all over" when he realized he might be looking at one of the "Bigfoot" creatures that had made headlines in recent years, and though he saw the potential value of the pictures, it was five years before the shop gave them to the press. On December 14th, 1965, the San Francisco Chronicle printed what was presumably the best shot under the headline "Is This the Dread Man-Animal?" Since then, it has become intimately familiar to most sasquatch enthusiasts.

The photo shows a distant dark figure in dense woods with a thick bulbous body, two arms, two legs, and ahead with no apparent neck. It would tend to remind one of a gorilla standing upright were it not for its North American origins.

I know of no one in the sasquatch field which has seen any of the other shots from Hamilton's roll of film. It would be very useful to study the figure's movements as it changed position, but for some reason- probably the absence of a witness to question- no one seems to have regarded this case as a very big deal despite the photo's frequent use in books. A hoax can not be entirely ruled out, but was

Zack Hamilton the type to perpetuate one? No one knows, as he has never been located (but nor do any investigators seem to have tried very hard to do so). The assistant manager commented, "I don't think an old woodsman could fake a thing like that," and indeed, the man made no effort to profit from his story.

The best known of the Zack Hamilton photos from Oregon's Three Sisters Wilderness in 1960.

What is certain is that the photo does not show a bear or other known North American animal, and while the range of subject from camera presents a detailed analysis, I tend to have positive feelings in this case. Others are likely to be less certain, but I have never seen the Hamilton photo directly labeled a hoax.

CONCLUSION: Tentative acceptance.

PHOTOGRAPHER: Allen Plaster
LOCATION: Lake Worth outside Fort Worth, Texas
DATE: Summer or Fall, 1969
APPEARS IN- "The Bigfoot Casebook" by Janet & Colin Bord; "Bigfoot: Opposing Viewpoints" by Norma Gaffron

For several months from summer to fall, numerous people reported seeing a seven-foot, 300-pound white-haired creature in the nature reserve at Lake Worth. Dubbed the Lake Worth Monster, it became such an attraction that on some nights in July, the road through the area was jammed with sightseers hoping for a glimpse of it; one night, it reportedly hurled an old tire 500 feet into a crowd of people, an unlikely feat of strength for a hoaxer in an ape suit. Author Sallie Ann Clarke, investigating the sightings, saw the creature break through a barbed-wire fence. On November 7th, Charles Buchanan claimed he was sleeping in the back of his pickup on the lakeshore when the beast grabbed him and threw him to the ground. He shoved a bag of leftover chicken into its mouth, and it retreated into the water, swimming toward Greer Island. With so many witnesses, it would have been surprising if no one had captured the Lake Worth Monster on film, and indeed a picture was taken by the owner of a local dress shop.

This is perhaps the ultimate example of the classic "fuzzy monster photo," obviously taken at night in a fit of great excitement without much time to focus. It shows a very large white body against a dark background, apparently standing in tall grass. One gets the impression of a profile shot, with a fairly small roundish head leaning slightly forward and just the hint of an arm going down what would be the left side, but there is no real detail to be made out. Still, just the extreme bulk would seem to rule out a man in a costume- or, alternately, if such a costume was used, it would have been so cumbersome that few if any of the witnesses would have failed to identify it as such.

CONCLUSION: Tentative acceptance.

PHOTOGRAPHER: Rosemary Tobash
LOCATION: Kootenay National Park, British Columbia
DATE: 1974
APPEARS IN: "The Mysterious Monsters" by Robert & Frances Guenette; "The Mysterious Monsters" (feature film)

Rosemary Tobash of East Cleveland, Ohio, supplied this photo to researcher Robert Guenette, saying she had taken it while on vacation. No other details of the story-

Allen Plaster's hazy shot of the Lake Worth Monster from 1969.

Rosemary Tobash's indistinct photo of something atop
a waterfall in Kootenay National Park, British Columbia,
in 1974.

Her feelings on the incident, whether the subject of the photo was moving or stationary, etc.- seem to have been recorded.

A dark figure is seen lying across the rocks on a cliff face next to a waterfall. Two arms and possible facial details, though vague, can be envisioned, but the distance is so great that it could just as easily be an oddly shaped patch of dirt. Guenette's comment was that the photo "fails to excite."

CONCLUSION: Inconclusive.

PHOTOGRAPHER: Anonymous
LOCATION: Near Chittenden, Vermont
DATE: October, 1976
APPEARS IN: "Monsters of the Northwoods" by Paul & Bob Bartholemew, William Brann, and Bruce Hallenbeck; "In the Shadow of Bigfoot" (commercial video)

Owned by investigators Jeff and Ted Pratt, this photo was taken by an anonymous businessman from Rutland, Vermont, on a nature trail in northeast Rutland County. He was photographing a bridge, but after the film was developed, a mysterious figure turned up in the background.

The figure is a solid black form vaguely shaped like a humanoid upper body, with one arm extended to the side. It is surrounded by dense woods and is quite high in the picture, but whether it would be on high ground or actually in the treetops is not clear. The bridge is in the foreground.

The picture has been offered as possible evidence for the presence of sasquatch in the area, and indeed there are several reports from the states of Vermont and New York. Examination of the site revealed no natural object that could have accounted for the strange form, and a professional analysis of the photo was reportedly inconclusive.

However, the supposed creature appears so featureless in an otherwise fairly detailed picture that the most likely explanation, by far, is that it is actually just a peculiar shadow effect produced by the branches and leaves, a one-chance-in-a-thousand illusion.

CONCLUSION: Natural formation.

PHOTOGRAPHER: Karl Blagge
LOCATION: Near Ukiah, Oregon (?)
DATE: September, 1977
APPEARS IN: The Track Record #32, October 1993

Blagge was involved in research work for the Department of Agriculture in the late 1970s. One day he was viewing a herd of mule deer from inside a truck ten miles northeast of Ukiah and took several pictures of them. Three of these captured an image in the truck's rear-view mirror of what he claimed was a sasquatch, 10-12 feet tall, standing between two trees a considerable distance away.

Vermont, October 1976. The dark "creature" at the top
is most likely just a product of leaves and shadows.

An enlargement made by Blagge and shown in vivid color in The Track Record, a newsletter of the Western Bigfoot Society of Portland, shows a vertical, slender, and vaguely manlike form with a very pointed head. No arms or legs are discernible, and it is apparently standing motionless.

Karl Blagge's September, 1977 view of something large
standing between two trees.

Without knowing the height of the trees, it is difficult to judge the
figure's size, and it is too far away to make out any detail at all.

(Note: Though The Track Record listed the state as Oregon, a
check of the map shows that Ukiah is actually in California.)

CONCLUSION: Inconclusive.

PHOTOGRAPHER: Unknown
LOCATION: Near Index/Monte Cristo, Washington
DATE: 1979
APPEARS IN: "Ancient Mysteries: Bigfoot" (t.v. series, A & E)

This is another example of a photograph without much of a story
to go with it. It is owned by investigator Cliff Crook of Bothell, Washington's "Bigfoot Central," who says he received it from the anonymous photographer. Apart from the approximate date and location,
the only detail released about the sighting was that it was of a

blonde-colored creature rising from a pond in the Cascade Mountains.

The photo is very enigmatic, showing what appears to be a broad-shouldered, light-haired figure up to its chest in water. The face has dark eyes with dark vertical streaks beneath them, but little else in the way of detail is apparent. The surrounding trees are reflected on the pond's surface.

Jon Eric Beckjord, a well-known figure in cryptozoological circles who has operated a small cryptozoology museum in Malibu, California, dismissed this photo in a letter as "a dummy in a pond." Beckjord is rather notorious for supporting photos and films that others denounce and for pointing out details in photos that no one else seems able to see. Him calling this one a fake would seem to have special significance. The "Ancient Mysteries" television series also labeled it a hoax. Is there a basis for this?

There is. The reflections on the water in the photo are undisturbed, suggesting a calm, flat surface. This could hardly be expected for a pond with a sasquatch (or any wild animal) standing or swimming in it. At least some small waves or ripples would surely be disturbing the surface, so the most likely explanation is probably Beckjord's- that an artificial object was placed in the water and photographed.

(It should also be noted that Index and Monte Cristo- both given as the area where the photo was taken- are not at all close to each other.)

CONCLUSION: Hoax.

OTHER PHOTOS FEATURED IN "ANCIENT MYSTERIES: BIGFOOT" ON THE ARTS & ENTERTAINMENT (A & E) CHANNEL:

This program featured a segment in which several still photos were flashed and some very brief data printed on screen with each, including the producers' evaluations.

There were no in-depth case histories given and no photographers named. The Index pond photo was one of these. Others were as follows:

WATERFALL FORKS, WASHINGTON- 1972
ANALYSIS: HOAX

This bizarre troll-like figure squatting before a body of water has no obvious arms or legs and shows a very vague face. Overall is looks entirely unsatisfactory.

MT. RAINIER, WASHINGTON: 1991
ANALYSIS: UNDETERMINED

A hulking black silhouette stands with its arms at its sides in forest surroundings. Widely publicized sightings and tracks in the Mt. Rainier area were investigated by Cliff Crook in the fall of 1990, so this is quite intriguing.

(Something crossing the figure's chest diagonally reminds me of a certain hairy character who wore an ammunition belt in the same position in "Star Wars," and I like to call this the "Chewbacca shot.")

BIGFOOT LAKE, WASHINGTON: 1978
ANALYSIS: TREE STUMP

A vaguely humanoid shape is seen in a thicket across a body of water and does look a lot like a strangely-shaped stump.

NORTH CASCADES, WASHINGTON: 1992
ANALYSIS: BEAR

I do not see a sasquatch or an obvious bear in this photo, but a dark something-or-other hugging the right-hand frame that is so close to the camera it is just a blob. However, it is hard to believe that the photographer could have mistaken a bear for a sasquatch at such close range, as it would have been almost upon him.

LOCATION UNKNOWN: 1993
ANALYSIS: HOAX

Bravo to "Ancient Mysteries" for this evaluation; though it's amazing, they would even feature this blatantly goofy full-color and broad daylight shot of a wooden carving of a sasquatch (or possibly of some kind of ape) down on all fours. Very good craftsmanship- but would you look at a photo of Michelangelo's David and think it was a real person?

There were also two hitherto unknown photos (along with that of Zack Hamilton) shown without comment or explanation during the narrative introduction to this segment. Both showed the vaguest solid black, two-legged silhouettes in dense forest and are totally useless as evidence, not even lending themselves to evaluation.

In addition, in an earlier part of the program, another pair of poor quality still photos was shown as well as part of a cine film showing a rather small creature with basic human proportions skulking away into the trees from a trail or clearing. All of this was simply flashed without comment during narration about the subject in general.

The bizarre Index, the Washington photo purports to show a light-colored creature rising from a pond but fails to give an impression of anything more than an inanimate model placed in the water.

Waterfall Forks, Washington, 1972. "Ancient Mysteries" Photos.

Mt. Rainier, Washington, 1991. Chewbacca lives!
"Ancient Mysteries" Photos.

Bigfoot Lake, Washington, 1978. "Ancient Mysteries"
Photos.

North Cascades, Washington, 1992. Attack of the Blob.
"Ancient Mysteries" Photos.

Location unknown, 1993. Nice try. "Ancient Mysteries"
Photos.

"Ancient Mysteries" Photos.

"Ancient Mysteries" Photos.

"Ancient Mysteries" Photos.

"Ancient Mysteries" Photos.

One frame from a cine film or video. Ancient Mysteries" Photos.

PHOTOGRAPHER: Bubba Williamson
LOCATION: Green Swamp near Auburndale, Florida
DATE: March, 1984

APPEARS IN- The Sun. November 27th, 1984, reprinted in The Bigfoot Record #2

Williamson, 21, and friend Flip Statler, 20, reportedly spotted a nine-foot sasquatch in an area of swamps and orange groves while hunting deer in the early part of 1984. Other sightings had been made the previous year. When the two saw the creature, they watched briefly until it ran away, but in March, they saw it or a similar one a second time behind some trees and managed to take a few photos before it again ran off. Afterward, they found footprints and scraps of fruit and vegetation on the ground.

The single picture printed in The Sun shows very little, just a dark bulbous shape partially concealed behind foliage in a swampy area. It can not be determined even if the supposed creature is in profile or facing directly toward or away from the camera, and it could easily be an inanimate object.

The Sun is one of the supermarket tabloids notorious for mixing true stories with total fiction; thus, it is hard to make a judgment call on this case. I will simply note that deer hunting seasons are generally in the fall, not the first three months of the year.

CONCLUSION: Inconclusive.

Now, a note about tabloids in general. Several alleged Bigfoot photos have turned up in those lovable pieces of supermarket aisle literature over the years. I remember one that supposedly showed a man who had run over a sasquatch with his truck and killed it, but the creature lying on the ground in front of the vehicle was obviously nothing but a drawing added to the photo. I could not locate that particular one, but let's take a look at a few of the more interesting ones from my collection:

In the October 10th, 1989 issue of the Weekly World News, an article appeared under the headline "BIGFOOT BABY FOUND!" It told of an infant creature captured by Dutch anthropologists in southwest China near the Burmese border on September 15th after its angry 8-foot tall mother was frightened away. As clearly shown in the accompanying photo, the male infant- only a few weeks old but weighing 32 pounds- had a very human-like face and was covered in thick brown hair. After only a short time in captivity, it had already learned to drink from a cup.

The photo is almost certainly a computerized creation, with a human child's face blended with God only knows what

That's not as dramatic as the monstrous beast that came raging out of the blue on the pages of The Sun on April 20th, 1993. Screaming headlines declared: "WORLD EXCLUSIVE! MOUNTAIN DRAMA AS BRAVE CLIMBER MEETS 700 POUNDS OF FIGHTING FURY! FIRST EVER PHOTOS OF BIGFOOT!" (First ever? I enjoy a good story as much as the next guy, but clearly, these tabloid journalists are living in their own private reality, especially since The Sun itself had already published the Bubba Williamson photo nine years earlier.)

Bubba Williamson's photo of Auburndale, Florida's "Creature from the Green Swamp," March 1984.

The story told how mountain climber Leonard Morton was chased by the creature while on a solo venture in Oregon and hid in a cave for eight hours as it tried to get at him. The pictures shown were said to be from a video he shot as it came closer to him. Also shown were its enormous 24-inch tracks (out of all proportion, since the creature itself was said to be "only" eight feet tall), which had a thumb-like toe such as is found in apes, totally unlike known sasquatch tracks.

And the creature itself? Straight out of a B-grade horror movie and about as fake as they come. A fat pear-shaped body covered in brown hair sits atop two impossibly short legs and is topped by a head about half the size of the body. The hairless but bearded face features glaring dark eyes and fierce barred teeth. The creature is flecked with snow as it appears in various poses. And that is exactly what they are- poses- as this is almost certainly a model placed in various positions and photographed, which would make the claim that these shots came from a video untrue. And to top it off, "Leonard Morton" is pictured with a tape measure showing the size of one of the tracks, and there is a barbed-wire fence behind him. How peculiar to find that in the middle of the wilderness.

That particular presentation was amusing enough, but somehow it showed up in a second incarnation in 1999. In the February 2000 issue of Bigfoot Times, investigator Daniel Perez describes how he was shown a blurry version of one of these same pictures (the one shown here) at the annual Sasquatch Symposium in Vancouver, British Columbia by Mr. and Mrs. Lloyd Sanders, who said that it was taken by a friend of theirs', "a good Christian woman." Perez identified it as the same one from The Sun, and wrote, "Whether Lloyd Sanders is the responsible party behind the fake, or his 'Christian' friend, remains to be seen."

So what happened to Leonard Morton?

A final tabloid production we'll look at here is probably the granddaddy of them all and actually caused quite a stir for a while among people who wondered if it could possibly be true. It appeared, once again, in that old favorite, the Weekly World News on April 23rd, 1991, under the headline "1st BIGFOOT CAPTURED!" and told of how a Dr. Leonard Owens and three assistants had bagged the beast with a tranquilizer dart near Deer Lodge, Montana. Several photos of the capture and of the awakened creature in captivity were shown- absolutely without question, a man in heavy makeup, looking somewhat like the character Vincent from the former t.v. series "Beauty and the Beast." It was supposed to have been darted from "a few hundred yards," when in reality, tranquilizer guns are effective only from extremely close range, and even a few hundred feet would be too far.

The creature was said to be at a research facility near Helena, but in later follow-up stories, it was reported that it had been flown to

Italy for scientific examination, where it had killed its guards and escaped. That seemed to be the end of this wild tale.

But on June 1st, 1999, WWN reran the exact same story- same text, same photos- as if it had just happened, totally ignoring how they had run it eight years before. I suppose they thought people would have forgotten by then.

The captured Bigfoot baby from China. Photoshop works wonders, doesn't it?

Yaaahh!!! Attack of the giant man-eating killer sasquatch from Hell! A tabloid at its best.

Weekly World News' captured sasquatch from Montana. A twice-told tale.

Dr. Leonard Owens, Leonard Morton, Dutch anthropologists in China... people named in the most fantastic of tabloid stories almost invariably turn out to be fictional characters. As for Bubba Williamson, that was much more of a mundane-type story with a typical enigmatic photo rather than one of these crystal-clear obvious fakes, so who knows? I have occasionally seen sasquatch stories in tabloids that I knew to be true, but all in all, they are hardly a reliable source of information on this or any other subject.

PHOTOGRAPHER: Anthony B. Wooldridge
LOCATION: Himalayas, Northern India
DATE: March 6th, 1986
APPEARS IN: BBC Wildlife. September 1986; The ISC Newsletter. Winter 1986; "Bigfoot: Opposing Viewpoints" by Norma Gafffon; "Mysterious Creatures," Time/Life Mysteries of the Unknown series

The Yeti or Abominable Snowman of the Himalayas has been strangely absent from the photographic history of cryptozoology, and did not make its first appearance until March of 1986 when Englishman Anthony Wooldridge was on a solo run in the mountains of northern India as part of Traidcraft, an organization supporting developing countries. On the 6th, he left the village of Govind Ghat at six a.m., hoping to reach Hemkund, in a region near the border of Nepal. At about 11,200 feet in elevation, he found strange 10-inch tracks in a steep wooded area that seemed to meander from bush to bush. Puzzled, he took a few pictures of them and then continued on. Half an hour later, he heard the sound of an avalanche in the distance, and reached its source at 12:30 p.m. at nearly 13,000 feet. A huge slide of wet snow blocked his path, and as he was attempting to negotiate it, he saw tracks leading from a "large, smooth groove" in the snow to a bush in the midst of the snowfield, behind which stood a dark figure over six feet tall.

Wooldridge had little interest in tales of the yeti, but figured that he must be looking at one and took several photos of the mysterious figure, unaware that he was the first person ever to do so. He watched it for about 45 minutes, during which time it remained stationary behind the bush, although the bush seemed to shake several times slightly and at least once the supposed yeti seemed to shift position-Wooldridge thought to keep him in its sight. The weather then began to worsen, and he left the scene at 1:30, descending to the village of

Pulna, but fearing his report might spark a hunt for the creature, he said nothing of it until his return to England.

Several British experts on the subject of the yeti had positive reactions to the report, but most significant was that of the late John Napier, world-renowned primate expert and author of the 1973 book "Bigfoot: The Yeti and Sasquatch in Myth and Reality." In that book, he had grudgingly accepted that the American sasquatch was probably real, "...but whether it is all that it is cracked up to be is another matter altogether." Evidence for the yeti, meanwhile, failed to impress him, and he tended to write the creature off as "... a red herring, or, at least, as a red bear." But upon seeing the Wooldridge evidence, Napier announced, "In my view, the creature in the photograph is a hominid... It is not human in the general sense of the word, although it may belong to the genus Homo... The creature cannot be anything but a Yeti..."

One of Anthony B. Wooldridge's March 6th, 1986 photos of a supposed yeti in northern India, with an enlargement of the object in question. Officially explained away as just a rock, there still seems to be at least some room for doubt.

The photos that so impressed Dr. Napier- one, in particular, that was subsequently published- show the figure about 500 feet from the camera on a steep, snow-covered rocky slope. Enlargements are able to bring out its shape- humanoid, with a squarish head, arms and shoulders of basic human proportions, and apparently up to its knees in deep snow- as well as the sparse bush it seems to be using unsuccessfully for concealment. It's dark coloring- unbroken by any variation- would seem to indicate a full-body coat of hair.

It was only the following year, however, and shortly after John Napier had passed away, that Wooldridge announced that thorough analysis of his photos- as well as comparison with others of the same scene he took in a return trip to the Himalayas- had revealed that the impressive looking "yeti" had in fact been only a large, strangely-shaped rock. Almost all cryptozoological publications quickly acknowledged the mistake, and the matter was quietly laid to rest.

There were some, however, who were less than convinced. Hadn't Wooldridge originally reported at least slight movements of the creature he watched? Then there was the matter of the tracks, which actually led straight to the strange figure from the snowslide. Also, none of the comparison photos that were supposed to clearly show the alleged rock were ever published. It wouldn't have been the first time, some said, that a person with such an experience had later recanted after extensive publicity out of job security fears or a desire for privacy.

Most experts will steadfastly disagree, but as long as a shadow of doubt remains, this case must remain open. It just seems so unlikely that the eminent Dr. Napier would reverse his skeptical stance on the very existence of the yeti simply by looking at pictures of a rock.

CONCLUSION: Inconclusive.

PHOTOGRAPHER: Charles Edson
LOCATION: Fremont area (?), California
DATE: Unspecified
APPEARS IN: "Those Incredible Animals" (t.v. series, Discovery)

"Those Incredible Animals" was a wildlife program geared mostly toward young people and hosted by actress Loretta Swit. One episode dealt with famous "monsters," and the segment on sasquatch centered on California Bigfoot hunter Charles Edson, who said he'd been on the creatures' trail since 1952 when giant footprints made him a believer. At first, he had hunted them with a gun but believed they could sense the weapon and had had several close sightings since abandoning it. As proof, the show presented brief shots of four or five separate filmings achieved by Edson.

There were two still frames, but whether they were part of cine films or simply photographs was not specified. One shows a solid black figure with more or less human proportions walking in a large clearing some distance from the nearest trees, facing either directly toward or directly away from the camera. The other is of a similar figure in profile, leaning back slightly with one leg extended forward, surrounded by trees but with bright sunlight in the background. (It is those two shots that are presented here.)

Photos by Charles Edson from the Fremont, California area.

Photos by Charles Edson from the Fremont, California area.

Then there were sections of at least two, possibly three cine films, all showing the familiar hulking black figure walking through dense forest. The closest to the camera seems particularly husky in its built but has a very brisk and bouncy walk as it moves away.

There was no comment given on each individual film, only the statement that they were all Charles Edson's. All have one thing in common- a dark figure too far away to show any real detail- thus, it is really impossible to make much of an evaluation of any of them. They may be a sasquatch, and they may not.

CONCLUSION: Inconclusive.

PHOTOGRAPHER: Unknown
LOCATION: Scape Ore Swamp near Bishopville, South Carolina
DATE: 1988
APPEARS IN: "Those Incredible Animals" (t.v. series, Discovery)

On the same episode featuring the films of Charles Edson from California, this program covered the famous "Lizard Man" story that made national headlines in the summer of 1988. This began when 16-year-old Chris Davis reported being attacked by a seven-foot, scaly, upright creature with three-fingered hands and red glowing eyes while changing a tire in the Scape Ore Swamp area at night. Other sightings followed, and three-clawed footprints were found, but the chaotic publicity surrounding the case and the inevitable wild tabloid-like claims capitalizing on the original reports quickly turned off most serious investigators. Still, some suspected the Lizard Man might actually be a swamp-dwelling sasquatch that only appeared scaly when wet and covered with swamp slime.

One investigator who stayed longer than most, living for a time in the area and exploring the swamp extensively, reported to the author in a phone conversation that one evening a local resident visited him and hesitantly told of his encounter with the creature while on the road en route with his grandson to a fishing spot. As proof, he produced a photograph, which he apparently had no interest in keeping, that showed- sure enough- what appeared to be not a scaly "Creature from the Black Lagoon" but a hair-covered figure somewhat resembling a sasquatch. The investigator planned to use this picture in a book he was preparing, but I know of no one who has seen this, and apparently, the project did not come to fruition.

But could this photo be the one shown ever-so-briefly on "Those Incredible Animals" with barely any commentary or explanation?

The T.V. crew was in the office of local sheriff Liston Truesdale who was shown looking through some of his files on the Lizard Man case. One small snapshot was shown in closeup. It showed an extremely vague and dark-colored something-or-other on a curving dirt road through a wooded area. It is short, possibly crouched down. As he holds the photo in his hand Sheriff Truesdale says, "Looks like it got mad, 'cause it didn't find what he wanted."

Possible photo of Lizard Man in South Carolina's Scape Ore Swamp. This was taken from a snapshot shown on t.v., with a man's thumb concealing the upper right corner.

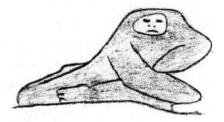

A suggestion for fleshing out the enigmatic shape seen in the Lizard Man photo. Just a possibility.

Jack Rowley's photo of a possible Alma creature in the former Soviet Union.

It is so vague it is useless, but interesting that the shape depicted resembles the Soviet hammer and sickle!

And that is all, no further comment. That is the problem with shows like this- they tend to condense great amounts of information into a loosely connected bunch of sound bytes, and we are left going, "Wait... what was that?"

CONCLUSION: Inconclusive.

PHOTOGRAPHER: Jack Rowley
LOCATION: Tien-Shan Mountains, Republic of Kirgizia
DATE: September, 1991
APPEARS IN: "The Legends Continue- Adventures in Cryptozoology" by Marc E.W. Miller

A group called New World Expeditions went on an expedition to a remote region on the border of China and central Asia to search for manlike creatures known locally as Almas, which are believed by some to be a survival of Neanderthal man. An American team was joined by several Russian mountaineers in their quest.

At one point, the remains of a rustic encampment were discovered, featuring shelters and primitive carvings, where it was thought a group of Almas may have lived at one time. On the same day, American Jack Rowley had another intriguing experience, as told in fellow team member Marc Miller's 1998 book:

"Jack Rowley had observed a strange human-like form nestled in distant rocks. Upon investigation, the shadowy figure had disappeared, but Jack had taken a photo of the strange human-like creature. Later we had the photograph enlarged for further examination. It showed a primitive appearing human form. This appeared to be a possible Alma lurking in the distance, foraging for food. Some hair specimens were also collected for further study."

The version of the photo shown in the book, however, is extremely indistinct and shows nothing discernible at all. One can only hope that the enlargement was as good as Miller describes it.

CONCLUSION: Inconclusive.

PHOTOGRAPHER: Unknown
LOCATION: Ohio (?)
DATE: 1992 (?)
APPEARS IN: Coshocton Tribune: North American Bigfoot Information Network Journal #5, Winter/Spring 1992; "World's Greatest Hoaxes- Secrets Finally Revealed" (t.v. special, FOX)

On February 4th, 1992, sasquatch investigator Doug McCoy of Bunker Hill, Indiana, received a videotape in the mail with no name or return address and no letter of explanation. The postmark was Coshocton, Ohio. As McCoy was on his way to visit

fellow investigator Art Kapa of Mayville, Michigan, he brought the tape along, and they watched it for the first time together.

To the mens' surprise, the tape showed an upright but otherwise gorilla-like creature covered with dark hair. About five minutes of footage (long for such a piece) showed the creature walking through snow-covered woods.

From the outset, McCoy and Kapa firmly believed the video to be a hoax, but admitted it was very well done and featured a quite realistic costume. They set about trying to discover who was responsible and where it had been filmed, copyrighting it under their own names and having two still frames printed in the Coshocton Tribune with an offer of $500 for anyone willing to come forward with proof. Several suspects were reportedly considered, but no final answers were ever found.

When the FOX special "World's Greatest Hoaxes" used the video in December of 1998- correctly labeling it a hoax though also very incorrectly lambasting the 1967 Patterson film- they pointed out how the supposed creature stays around for a long time to have its picture taken, not how a real wild animal generally behaves. I have never heard anyone say they thought this video was genuine.

CONCLUSION: Hoax.

PHOTOGRAPHER(S): Robert Daigle and others
LOCATION: Ohio
DATE: Summer, 1992 (Unpublished)

A Michigan man, Robert Daigle, related the following in a letter in August of 1993:

"I have lots of video footage of Bigfoot activity taken in the summer of '92 in Ohio: thrown rocks, waving tree branches, glowing eyes, a small abandoned house being broken apart from the inside (shot at night from 300 ft. by a camera left running for 3 hrs, aided by lights activated by a motion detector), and about 6 sec. of bright daylight footage taken at 300 ft. by accident by a friend of mine (didn't zoom in)... shows 3 apparent creatures.

"Don Keating has made still photos of my video footage showing one black creature."

In another letter in May of 1998, he added:

"I have a less-than-a-minute video taken by someone in Michigan in which several people, when carefully watching the tape, believe they see a creature mostly hidden by a tree, but I can't make it out myself."

Eastern Ohio sasquatch investigator Don Keating has written about a video shot by a female associate of Daigle's. On August 2nd, 1992, she was shooting some random footage of an area in which sasquatch activity had been reported. Apparently, nothing

Unusual, it wasn't noticed at the time, but the tape turned out to show a tall black figure appearing from behind a parked car and walking from left to right in a rather hunched-over manner. It is in sight long enough to take twelve steps and is 150 or 200 feet from the camera.

One poor image from the "abandoned house" video was included with Daigle's letter, the only one of these examples I have personally seen. It was labeled: "Xerox of still photo taken from a video. The head, arm, and part of the back of a white Sasquatch bending over to pick up an object on the floor. Taken with an 8x.l lux video camera and 150-watt floodlight triggered by an infrared motion detector.

Camera approx. 300 ft. from the subject." The Digital readout on the video reads 10:07 p.m., June 6th, 1992. The supposed creature, however, is represented only by a couple of white spots in a darkened doorway.

Hoax video from Ohio, sent anonymously to investigator Doug McCoy in 1992 and later featured on FOX television's "World's Greatest Hoaxes- Secrets Finally Revealed." This reproduction was done from a poor photocopy; the actual video is actually quite clear.

CONLUSION: Inconclusive.

PHOTOGRAPHERS: Daryl Owen and Scott Herriott
LOCATION: Klamath area, Northern California
DATE: October 12th, 1992
APPEARS IN: "Ancient Mysteries: Bigfoot" (t.v. series, A & E)

The prelude to this incident began at about 11:30 a.m. on September 12th, 1992, when two boys, ages eight and twelve, were in the woods near Klamath looking for snakes. Instead, they encountered a "big hairy man" that smelled "like rotten chicken," shaking a branch in its hand. They ran home and told the younger boy's father, Daryl Owen, who doubted their story but went to check it out. Giant manlike footprints 16 1/2 inches long and crashing noises in the brush made him a believer. Owen contacted Bigfoot enthusiast, comedian, and part-time actor Scott Herriott of Los Angeles, and the two spent three days examining the scene, finding some mysterious strands of brown hair.

Strange screams described as "bellowing, monkey-sounding

screeches" were heard the night after the boys' sighting and continued for several nights, echoing through the forested canyon behind the Owens' home. More than one creature seemed to be calling back and forth. Owen himself had a sighting during this period of a creature with long flowing hair on its head and a "dark burnt-orange colored face."

Scott Herriott returned on October 12th, and the two men entered the woods armed with camcorders. Their videos show that at first, they were filming each other as they made their way through very thick underbrush, but at around a quarter to three in the afternoon in this dense thicket, they then saw something huge in size with glowing red eyes peering at them through the brush, and both men filmed it.

The resulting footage (excerpts of which shown on television are apparently from Herriott's camera) was about ten minutes long and, being lit by bright sunshine penetrating the woods, does definitely seem to show something alive, hairy, and of large size. It is 35 to 40 feet from the cameras, and because of the concealing brush, no exact shape is evident, but it is beige in color, and though remaining in one spot, it does make slight movements. There is also the red-eye glow that Herriott said he first thought might be an inanimate reflectivity of some kind until the head started to sway back and forth.

From Robert Daigle's collection- an alleged white sasquatch breaks into an abandoned house in Ohio.

What seems to be an arm is also seen to swing slightly below the head. The overall impression is of a looming figure, vaguely seen but powerful in its very presence, staring the men down.

The moment was extremely emotional. Herriott's voice on the tape is heard to whisper, "...It's looking right at me. Holy s___. It's a sasquatch, man. I got it on f___ tape, I can't even f___ believe this; it's looking right back at us." Owen, meanwhile, said that after 29 seconds, he started to cry and couldn't hold on to his camera any longer.

The "Ancient Mysteries" T.V. show devoted a major segment to this case and arranged for Fleet Street Pictures, a commercial post-production film lab in Santa Monica, to analyze the video. This analysis, plus laser prints Daryl Owen had made from the tapes, brought out a few sharper details not evident before. If one looked hard enough, one could now make out the vague form of a creature lying down (perhaps a nocturnal beast bedded down for the day in this dense thick-et?) with its legs running horizontally to the right, kneecaps and toes some-what visible.

Daryl Owen & Scott Herriott's video of something staring back at them through thick brush in the Klamath area. California on 10/12/92.

But that's just it, in this case, really- "somewhat visible." There is something alive there, without a doubt, but a scene with Owen pointing at one of his prints and saying, "You can't see the eyes, but the eyes are right here" seems to be a perfect summation of the usefulness of his and Herriott's videos. These prints have bodily outlines drawn in, which would be completely lost on just about all observers otherwise. To make the case even hazier, Owen at one point calls the creature a "gorilla-looking man," but later refers to the creature with female pronouns.

More recently, Scott Herriott has capitalized on the publicity surrounding the event with a humorous mock-documentary film, "Journey Toward Squatchdom," and has hosted the t.v. series "Walt Disney World Inside Out." He is careful, however, to disassociate the Klamath videos from his comic parodies, as he says, "...because I am serious about that. I really think there was one of those things there."

I do too. I believe Owen and Herriott did film a sasquatch that day, but unfortunately, the thick tangle of brush it had bedded down in concealed it far too well for the resulting videos to ever convince skeptics.

CONCLUSION: Tentative Acceptance.

PHOTOGRAPHER: Unknown
LOCATION: Eastern Washington (?)
DATE: Early 1993 (?)
APPEARS IN: "Sightings" (t.v. series, FOX)

On May 7th, 1993, the "Sightings" series featured a segment on sasquatch reports from an area in eastern Washington near the Idaho border, filmed earlier in the year. It contained a videotape sent to the show anonymously with a Washington postmark after their investigation in the area had been completed.

The tape showed a brown-haired creature walking through a moderately dense forest. Its face, though not seen clearly, is hairless. It seems to be fairly close to the cameraman, walking in profile first from left to right, disappearing behind some trees.

The Hoax video was shown on FOX television's "Sightings" in 1993, anonymously sent in from eastern Washington. This still frame does not do justice to capturing what is seen in the full video and how obviously fake the costume is.

Then reappearing and walking right to the left, pausing at one point to turn and look toward the camera. It seems to be about man-sized and moves with a slow human-like gait.

Photo analyst Mike Stusser was featured on the show giving a positive opinion of the film, pointing out how the creature turns its entire upper body instead of just its head when looking toward the camera, much like an ape and like the creature in the Patterson Bigfoot film.

A different opinion was given by the International Society of Cryptozoology secretary J. Richard Greenwell, interviewed after the segment by series host Tim White. He said the film was "probably a hoax," but one gets the impression he was being kind even with that evaluation. A clear film in conjunction with very good eyewitness testimony, he said, would be much more convincing. "Otherwise, when it's a videotape that comes in, you don't know who took it, or it's questionable... has very little value."

That this video shows a human being in a costume is fairly obvious. At one point, light is seen reflecting off the bottom of one foot, as if it is made of shiny vinyl or plastic. The walk is stiff and slow, not at all-natural, a fact noted by Greenwell. The fact that the "creature" turns its body like the Patterson creature is not very significant when one considers that even if it is not just a fluke, this movement has been widely described before in published sources available to any potential hoaxer. (And in some of the cheaper gorilla suits, the masks are so loose-fitting that one's head will turn inside them, rather than the mask moving with the head.) As hoaxes go, this is not even a very good one.

(Incidentally, this segment on "Sightings" also showed two of the photos featured on A & E's "Ancient Mysteries- Bigfoot," not commented on at all in either program.)

CONCLUSION: Hoax.

PHOTOGRAPHER: Steven Williams
LOCATION: Near Molalla, Oregon
DATE: July 27th, 1993
APPEARS IN: The Track Record #32, October 1993

A family named Riddle reported sighting a sasquatch while camping along the Molalla River about 20 miles south of Molalla. Peter Byrne of the Oregon-based Bigfoot Research Project passed on the report to Ray Crowe of the Western Bigfoot Society in Portland, who in turn asked enthusiast Steve Williams to go and check it out. Williams accidentally captured a facelike image on film while photographing some of the people present.

The photo shows two women and two children, Teresa & Christopher Williams and Laura & Kaitlen Riddle, sitting comfortably and smiling, unaware of the figure mostly concealed in the trees behind them, which Steve Williams also did not see at the time. The face is vaguely baboon-like in appearance. In the original print, it appeared green, identical to the coloring of the trees and thus seeming to be just a product of leaves and shadows, but this was later revealed as a color blending error in the film processing lab. Subsequent computer analysis supposedly indicated an actual object.

Hello, what's this? Taken by investigator Steven Williams, this photo shows Teresa & Christopher Williams and Laura & Kaitlen Riddle sitting happily in the foreground and something resembling a baboon's face peering at them from the trees behind them. Taken near Molalla, Oregon, on July 27th, 1993.

Teresa and Christopher are also supposed to have seen the creature at night while at the site, adding weight to the story. Steve reported that the automatic rewind on his camera suddenly activated when he took the picture, leading to speculations on the supposed malfunction of machinery in the presence of sasquatch, sometimes reported by those with a psychic theory of the creatures' nature. (The Track Record, a newsletter of the Western Bigfoot Society, sometimes carries stories of this kind but warns readers to remember to "wear their skepticals.")

All theories aside, we are left with a very vague image.

CONCLUSION: Inconclusive.

ADDENDUM: An article by Ray Crowe in the February 1994 issue of The Bigfoot Co-Op newsletter mentioned further goings-on at the Molalla campground the previous month, including two photos taken by a woman named Sharon Jones of a kneeling brown-haired creature in some brush seen by her and a friend. The Jones family was apparently associated with the Riddles. Crowe wrote that he had not yet seen the photos, and the Co-Op did not mention them again in subsequent issues.)

PHOTOGRAPHER: D.S.
LOCATION: Devils Lake State Park, Wisconsin
DATE: First week of January, 1994 (Unpublished)

A man with the initials D.S. and his girlfriend were cross-country skiing in the state park about 35 miles north of Madison. He decided to photograph some of the scenery and saw nothing unusual at the time, but after the film was developed, a friend pointed out a strange figure in one shot.

The figure is possibly 50 to 100 yards from the camera, depending on the type of lens used, standing at the side of a snowy trail leading out of a dense thicket of evergreen and birch trees. It is grayish in color and appears to have two arms and two legs, a thick body, wide shoulders, and a large pointed head. The arms hang straight down, reaching the knees, the legs are rather short but not overly so, and the neck is short to nonexistent. No facial detail is clear. The figure is facing the camera but turned slightly to its left, standing motionless with two sets of ski tracks visible going right past it. With these for comparison, it may stand as tall as seven to eight feet.

Puzzled, D.S. showed the photo to wildlife officials near his home in Illinois, who thought it showed either an upright bear or a log. Unsatisfied with this, he returned to the spot in the park and found no natural object to account for the figure. About a week after taking the photo, he contacted sasquatch investigator Tim Olson of Bloomington, Minnesota (now living in Arcata, California), my partner in producing The Sasquatch Report newsletter at the time, who passed the report on to me.

The photo definitely shows something of great interest, especially since D.S. was a disbeliever in sasquatch previously and had no interest in the subject. I am usually very wary of these cases where something "just shows up on the film," but this figure is so clearly outlined and matches the general description of sasquatch so distinctly.

A photo was taken by a cross-country skier in January 1994 of what may very well be a sasquatch in Wisconsin. Enlargement shows the detail of the creature.

If it is not a hoax, it almost has to be the real thing. D.S. and his girlfriend had to have passed within feet of it without seeing it before it stepped out onto the trail behind them, and may not have seen it when taking the picture due to the distance and its coloring blending with that of the trees.

CONCLUSION: Tentative acceptance.

PHOTOGRAPHER: Anonymous
LOCATION: Mt. Baker-Snoqualmie National Forest, Washington
DATE: July 11th, 1995
APPEARS IN- The Columbian. December 15th, 1995, reprinted in Bigfoot Record #16; "Glimpses of Other Realities Vol. 2- High Strangeness" by Linda Moulton Howe; Postcard produced by Cliff Crook

Investigator Cliff Crook reportedly paid $1600 to a forestry worker for seven-color snapshots said to be of a sasquatch seen north of Ashford and southwest of Mt. Rainier, at a lagoon along a branch of Wild Creek. The witness, who chose to remain anonymous, said he first heard heavy splashing about 25 feet below him while out hiking, then saw the creature standing in the water and photographed it.

The one photo published (presumably the best?), known popularly as the "Wild Creek Photo," shows the alleged creature at very close range and in fairly good focus. The gray-haired body is enormous, the legs almost impossibly short, the arms extremely long. A face with deep sunken eyes peers out from entirely below the broad shoulders. The depth of the water is not clear but could not be very deep as it is just off the bank, and a sunken log is visible through the surface just behind the creature.

Newell Burton, president of Omega Photo Specialists in Bellevue, Washington, examined the photos and commented, "It's hard to create a situation to duplicate it, but it wouldn't be too difficult for someone who knows how to use the camera. The odds are they're not real, but who knows?"

Gordon Kyle of Overlake Photo, also in Bellevue, stated that the image was not cropped from another photo and added, "It's seamless, but then again, who can say that this isn't a posed model?"

Not me. Despite the extensive attention given to this case, I don't feel the proportions of this creature look at all-natural or that they are entirely the result of the odd downward angle at which the photos were taken. Also, as in the 1979 photo owned by Crook of a creature in a pond near Index, Washington, there seems to be no discernible disturbance to the water's surface despite the report of heavy splashing moments before. The most likely explanation to me is that the photographer used some sort of full-sized inanimate model.

1995's infamous Wild Creek Photo, owned by Cliff Crook. A massive beast or just a beastly mass?

CONCLUSION: Hoax.

PHOTOGRAPHER: Craig Miller
LOCATION: Jedediah Smith Redwoods State Park, Northern California
DATE: August 28th, 1995
APPEARS IN- "Hard Copy: The Playmate and the Primate" (t.v. series); "The Tonight Show with Jay Leno" (t.v. series, NBC); Idaho

State Journal. November 28th, 1995; Idaho State University News & Notes. December 11th, 1995: Bigfoot Record #16

We have here a case so tailor-made for publicity and sensation-alism that the positive opinions it elicited from many investigators came as a bit of a surprise.

At just past 8:30 p.m. on the evening in question, a 34-foot RV was making its way down Walker Road in the redwood forest northeast of Crescent City, California. Onboard were five members of a film crew employed in shooting a cable t.v. series, "Adventures." By all accounts, they were relaxing and enjoying themselves at the time, laughing and having a few beers, and cameraman Craig Miller was casually filming with a Sony camcorder. What brought their experience the most press, however, was that among them was Anna-Marie Goddard from Holland, Playboy magazine's 40th-anniversary Playmate.

(I recall writing once in an editorial for The Sasquatch Report newsletter that perhaps what the field of sasquatch study needed was a major sighting by a celebrity, but this was not quite what I had in mind. Now, of course, we also have Yosemite National Park serial killer Cary Anthony Stayner, who was known to be fascinated with Bigfoot, claimed to have seen the creature in the park and even used it as a topic of conversation to approach one of his victims in 1999. That was not what I had in mind either.)

As the group playacted and clowned for the camera, the driver-Anna-Marie's husband Colin Goddard- suddenly spotted something in the road ahead. "Look, you guys, a bear," he announced. Miller then came forward and aimed the camera out the windshield, and a confused mix of voices on the tape-recorded the group's reactions to what happened next.

"It's a bear... that's not a bear... oh, I don't know."

"Whooo, it looks like a big bear; let's go get it."

"Colin, turn your brights on."

COLIN: "It's a sasquatch, oh my god, we got a complete... Oh my god!"

The vehicle stopped as the figure went out of sight, and some of the witnesses got

out.

"No, we shouldn't go outside, this is sketchy."

"Come on, get out here, bring that fire, extinguisher... whatever it is, it's gone."

ANNA-MARIE: "Let's go inside, guys. I'm serious, let's get outta here."

(This is apparently censored dialogue, as the original tape was said to contain considerable profanity.)

The subject of the now-famous video is described as eerily similar in appearance to the 1967 Patterson sasquatch, which was filmed about 30 miles away. Seen in rainy, misty conditions and in the glare of headlights, it crosses the road, pauses directly in front of the RV, then disappears behind a tree. The segment is 27 seconds long, but the creature is only visible for about five seconds, and having viewed it on the Internet, I can say that there is also an extreme sense of the forward movement of the vehicle combined with the horizontal movement from left to right of the creature. Estimates using a visible notch in the tree put its height at just under eight feet (larger than the female creature in Patterson's film). The body is massive, covered in "matted and black" hair, and slouches slightly forward in a walk showing considerable bending of the knees. The head comes to a crest on top, with a sloping forehead and the chin well below the level of the shoulders. Colin Goddard also described high cheek-bones, a scruffy beard, and said it looked like it had "age under its belt." Most unusual of all, though, was a clearly visible erect male organ, a feature very seldom reported in any sasquatch sightings.

Reactions to the video were naturally varied. To many- even those within the sasquatch field- the case had "hoax" written all over it. The road, running through a popular state park, was extensively traveled. The witnesses were involved in the entertainment industry, sought publicity, and it was learned that the subject of Bigfoot had dominated their conversation just the night before. There was also the unlikelihood of having a camcorder out and running at the moment a sasquatch appears. And perhaps most ironic of all, FOX t.v. had recently aired the notorious "Alien Autopsy" film. Time, then, for tabloid t.v. to create a new Bigfoot film as well? Was it really possible that their story was true?

Reporter Mike McKenzie-Bahr, who had been with the group earlier the day of the filming, stated that they were always filming something or other, so having the camera handy was not unusual. And, of course, having a prior interest in something should not count against a person's claim of actually encountering it. This reasoning was also used against Roger Patterson, and by such a token science demands hard evidence from sasquatch hunters but will never accept it if they do produce it simply because of their previous interest. The real test of this report had to be the video itself.

Dr. Jeff Meldrum, an anthropologist and primate expert at Idaho State University in Pocatello and member of the Bigfoot Field Researchers' Organization, tentatively accepted the film as genuine. In studying it, he saw muscles contracting in the proper places for a real animal, not like the padding of a costume, and a "classic primate penile display" similar to what is seen in chimpanzees.

Investigator Daniel Perez of the Center for Bigfoot Studies in Norwalk, California, took on the case as a skeptic, but after extensive studies at the film site and talking to most of the parties involved, he too came to accept it as genuine. "I still support the film 100%," he stated in a March, 1998 letter, and in the August 2000 issue of his Bigfoot Times newsletter he marked the fifth anniversary of the film by presenting the recent findings of video expert Dave Bittner from Pixel Workshop, Inc. "I've watched the video hundreds of times," he wrote to Perez, "at every possible speed, with various forms of magnification and digital enhancement, and I've yet to see anything in it that points to a hoax." Perez is known for his strict, no-nonsense approach, and his endorsement would seem to carry considerable weight. Veteran investigator John Green, meanwhile, is slightly less positive but wrote, "I have never heard of any proof one way or the other. It certainly looks possible."

This case, then, was a surprise in more ways than one, and it seems to have withstood the many strikes it had against it.

One frame from the famous video shot by Craig Miller in the California redwoods in the company of Playboy centerfold Anna-Marie Goddard. As it was shot in rainy conditions, the light areas are headlight glare. The object in the lower right corner is the front seat of the RV in which the witnesses were riding. (1995)

A frame from the Danny Sweeten video from Sam Houston National Forest in Texas. (1995)

CONCLUSION: Tentative acceptance.

PHOTOGRAPHER: Danny Sweeten
LOCATION: Sam Houston National Forest, Texas
DATE: October 5th, 1995
APPEARS IN- "Strange Universe" (t.v. show)

"Strange Universe" showed a video shot by Sweeten, a gunsmith by trade, reportedly of a large male sasquatch walking through some woods in San Jacinto County in southeast Texas.

Investigator Cliff Crook of Bothell, Washington's Bigfoot Central, in Bigfoot Trails Newszine #1, Jan-Feb 1998, wrote:

"Re: The Texas film, we received some information behind it, which sent it directly to the hoax file shortly after its release. Directors decided to keep that information mum in some interest of a future report/announcement."

Others, however, seem to support this rather far off footage of a basic black creature seen through thick tree cover. Regardless, it is too vague to prove anything.

CONCLUSION: Inconclusive.

PHOTOGRAPHER: Julie Ellif
LOCATION: Chilliwack/Agassiz area, British Columbia
DATE: May 5 or 6, 1997
APPEARS IN- "In Search of Giants: Bigfoot Sasquatch Encounters" by Thomas Steenburg

Two tourists from Somerset, England- Wayne Oliver and his girl-friend Julie Ellif- were on a driving tour of British Columbia and Alberta. They were driving along the TransCanada Highway with Oliver at the wheel and Ellif videotaping scenery, and as they approached the town of Hope (but were closer to Chilliwack and Agassiz), Oliver was singing but turned away from the camera in embarrassment. As he did, he caught sight of something in an open area off the highway, a dark upright figure moving toward a slough from a stand of trees, and called Ellif s attention to it.

In the resulting video, Ellif is heard to exclaim, "Sasquatch!"

"What's that?" Oliver responds.

"Sasquatch!"

The figure appears on the tape for only about five seconds. As there was considerable traffic on the highway, it was difficult for them to turn around for another look, so they just kept going. Upon their return to England, Oliver became very intrigued with what they had seen and filmed, having been interested in the creature before and now amazed that he may have been able to see one on his very first visit to Canada. After doing some research, he contacted investigator Thomas Steenburg of Alberta and sent him the tape.

Unfortunately, enlargements Steenburg had made at the University of Calgary distorted the image on the tape, and only an unidentifiable dark blur could be made out. It was concluded, however, that the couple had seen and filmed an animate upright object. Whether it was a sasquatch or a man is still in question.

Veteran investigator John Green went to the site of the incident, later writing to Steenburg:

"There was nothing there to account for the figure in the video while we were studying the area, but when we stopped there on the way back, there was, a human standing on the beach at the far side of the slough. That was at dusk, and the figure just looked black. Presumably, it would be a person fishing. At that location, I would say the odds would be 1000 to 1 that any upright walking figure would be a person rather than a Sasquatch, unless they had a clear enough look at it to be sure it could not have been human."

Oliver was emphatic, however, that what he and Ellif saw was not a human being.

In the frame from the video shown here, I am not at all sure exactly where the figure in question is supposed to be. As in so many other cases, you be the judge.

CONCLUSION: Inconclusive.

PHOTOGRAPHER: Vince Doerr

LOCATION: Ochopee, Florida
DATE: 1997
APPEARS IN: The Internet

(In the interest of long-term reference, web addresses will not be given since many have only a limited lifespan.)

"Skunk Ape" sightings in Florida had slacked off considerably when the creature suddenly seemed to make a comeback in 1997. After a guided tour group at Ochopee saw a large apelike animal at the edge of a swamp, Ochopee fire chief Vince Doerr saw the same or a similar creature cross a road near his home. He managed to take a quick snapshot of it before it disappeared into the swamp.

This first-ever Skunk Ape photo (unless you count John Sohl's from 1975, which didn't turn out see next chapter) caused a flurry of publicity, but Doerr himself believed he had only photographed a prankster in a furry costume. "I just think someone's playing games," he said. "I just looked at it and laughed. If I thought it was real, I would have run in there, beat it to death, and sold it to the National Enquirer."

The photo shows a brown humanoid shape surrounded by trees and swamp grass, without much other detail apparent. It would have to be a very determined hoaxer, though, to charge into such difficult terrain while wearing an ape suit.

One frame from the video shot by English tourist Julie Ellif in May, 1997 in British Columbia. Where is the alleged sasquatch? It's there somewhere.

Vince Doerr's photo from Ochopee, Florida in 1997- is it a Skunk Ape in a swamp or a costumed hoaxer?

CONCLUSION: Inconclusive.

PHOTOGRAPHER: Dave Shealy
LOCATION: Florida Everglades
DATE: November, 1997
APPEARS IN: The Internet

(In the interest of long-term reference, web addresses will not be given since many have only a limited lifespan.)

1997 was definitely the year for the Skunk Ape. Dave Shealy, owner of the Florida Panther Gift Shop in Ochopee and operator of a "Skunk Ape research center," had been regularly staking out an area in the Everglades by laying out lima beans as bait and sitting in wait in a tree. Finally, one night, his patience paid off. He had dozed off for a while, then awoke to see a creature coming straight toward him and took an amazing 27 photographs from about 50 yards away.

Shealy said he never felt afraid of the 7-foot creature. "After taking the photos," he said, "I sat back and took a deep breath and thought what a docile, docile animal was out there." He has appeared on several t.v. programs and in worldwide tabloids discussing his Skunk Ape experiences, and has promised more searching.

The picture shown here shows the creature running through swamp grass with trees in the background. As in most such cases, it is too dark to make out any details. In light of certain background information on Shealy himself, however (see below), a hoax seems likely.

CONCLUSION: Hoax.

ADDENDUM: Shealy claimed another photographic encounter with the skunk ape on July 8th, 2000, producing a short videotape segment that was shown on several T.V. news programs. The time stamp on the tape shows that it was shot at 7:21 p.m., and it shows a thin black silhouetted figure running through virtually identical terrain to the earlier set of photos. In the July 2000 issue of Bigfoot Times, investigator Daniel Perez wrote, "Having seen the footage, my first instinct is that it is a costumed man trying to run in an exaggerated fashion. David Shealy claims three sightings, and the rumor mill indicates his credibility is highly questionable."

On the website for the Bigfoot Field Researchers' Organization, Shealy is called an "ex-convict... a pathetic charlatan desperado in south Florida" with "a long track record as a hoaxer." It also mentions how he has sought funding for tourist promotions centered on his skunk ape stories and points out how all the evidence is "usually plentiful around his roadside gift shop and RV park in Ochopee, Florida." It would not be surprising, it seems, to hear an accusation that the Vince Doerr photo from Ochopee was actually of Shealy himself in an ape suit.)

PHOTOGRAPHER: Mary Green (?)
LOCATION: Tennessee
DATE: February, 1998
APPEARS IN: The Internet

Dave Shelay's first filming experience in the Florida
Everglades in November, 1997 (from a series of 27
photos).

Closeup of supposed sasquatch face in Tennessee
photo by Mary Green. It is darkened somewhat to
sharpen details. The arrow points to the straight line of
the mouth.

(In the interest of long-term reference, web addresses will not be
given since many have only a limited lifespan.)

An extremely enigmatic photo can be found on the Internet
under the heading 'Tennessee Bigfoot Lady." Mary Green is part of
an organization called the GCBRO (I don't know what it stands for,
but I'm going to take a flying guess that it's probably the something-

something-Bigfoot Research Organization), and she describes the photo as showing up to four separate Bigfoot creatures hiding in the woods. To all initial appearances, it is a picture of nothing but the woods, but Green has drawn in the outlines of where she claims the creatures are.

As the photo is full of tangled brush and not much more, I have not done a rendering of the entire thing, only of a supposed face belonging to the most "visible creature. A branch covers part of the face on the right, and an arrow points to the horizontal line of the mouth. It should also be noted that this picture has been darkened to sharpen some of the vague details.

Green states that at first, only this one creature was visible in the picture, but that close study revealed up to three more. She also says that she or any other member of the GCBRO is prepared to take a lie-detector test at any time to prove the validity of their claims, but of course, that would not prove that there are sasquatches in the picture, only that they believe there are.

To me, it looks like a picture of woods. A person could take any such picture and imagine all sorts of images from the tangle of branches and shadows.

CONCLUSION: Natural formation.

PHOTOGRAPHER: Chad W. Michael
LOCATION: Unknown
DATE: November 24th, 1998
APPEARS IN: The Internet

(In the interest of long-term reference, web addresses will not be given since many have only a limited lifespan.)

This extremely unique home video turned up on the Internet, giving the date and the person's name but no location. Michael states that he had gone out on this late November day to roll up some garden hoses for the winter, and when he got to the hilltop where his garden was located, he saw a sasquatch walking through a nearby hayfield. He ran back to his house to fetch his video camera and got back in time to see the creature crouched down beside a white dome-shaped box that served as a cover for a gas well in the field. Inside the box, a cat was napping, and experienced a very rude awakening.

The creature then proceeded to chase the cat, darting back and forth, diving for it, and missing and rolling on the ground. The cat itself is just visible in the footage, bounding for its life. But finally, while running straight toward the camera but still at a considerable distance, the creature makes one final dive and succeeds in catching its dinner. It rises to its knees, and as it brings its hands up to its mouth, the limp cat can be seen dangling.

Michael writes, "As I was filming this, I thought to myself, 'No way can he catch that cat.' I was wrong. I lost a cat but gained a great film."

As backup evidence, photos of the creature's 17" footprints are also shown.

Is it for real? The creature looks and moves like a person in a gorilla suit (and the Bigfoot Field Researchers' Organization website calls the video "one recent one where some clown in an ape costume chases around after a house cat on a lawn"), but more significant is the fact that the cat does actually appear to be killed. If it is a hoax, it is quite a sadistic one.

CONCLUSION: Inconclusive.

PHOTOGRAPHERS: Jim Smith/Anonymous Internet User
LOCATION: Lakeport, Florida
DATE: March 20th, 2000
APPEARS IN: The Internet

(In the interest of long-term reference, web addresses will not be given since many have only a limited lifespan.)

One more photo came about in the aftermath of the 1997 Skunk Ape fever. Jim Smith and his wife operate a fish camp and bar at Lakeport on the western edge of Lake Okeechobee in an area where several sightings have occurred and where the creature has very affectionately been named the "Okeechobee Ogre." Smith himself claims to have seen it more than once and says it often comes around his camp to feed on discarded fish guts. By September of 1998, the creature had become so popular that souvenirs were being sold in its name, and Smith claimed his camp as "Skunk Ape Central."

Smith then established what has became known on the Internet as the "Okeechobee Ogre Live Freak Cam," a camera set up behind his camp and pointing into the woods, transmitting a new live image every sixty seconds to anyone around the world who wants to log on and watch for the Ogre to appear. As one would expect, all anyone usually sees is a monotonous shot of the trees. But on the night of March 20th, 2000, a female net surfer was watching the Freak Cam and captured an image of something standing in the shadows.

The image is extremely faint, and no evaluation of any kind can really be made about it, but this may be the first and only time that a sasquatch has appeared live in the media. Aaah, modem technology.

CONCLUSION: Inconclusive.

PHOTOGRAPHER: Unknown
LOCATION: Near Mammoth Mountain, California, but claimed to be the Himalayas
DATE: Unknown
APPEARS IN: "World's Greatest Hoaxes- Secrets Finally Revealed" (t.v. special, FOX); "Paranormal Borderline" (t.v. show, UPN)

Frames from the "Bigfoot kills cat" video. When viewed in full, the cat can be seen bounding along, and the final frame here is of its demise. Probably a particularly vicious hoax.

Webcam shot of the Okeechobee Ogre, a Florida skunk ape. In the original, the supposed creature is so vague, appearing almost ghost-like; it is shown here only as a white outline.

It seems a shame to close this chapter with a definite disappointment, but this final video has indeed been revealed as a hoax. As mentioned earlier in the Patterson film chapter, it purported to show a Himalayan yeti cavorting about on a snowy slope and was originally said to have been taken by a European couple on a mountaineering vacation. The dark, shaggy creature is facing away from the camera as it trudges uphill and is shown only in quick, blurry images. This seems quite puzzling since the range is fairly close, and the cameraman should have had no trouble focusing and keeping the creature continuously in sight. There was also the fact that some of the foliage seen in the video looks suspiciously American, not Asian.

It became known popularly as the "Snow Walker" footage and raised some serious interest when it first appeared on the t.v. show "Paranormal Borderline." Dr. Jeff Meldrum of the Bigfoot Field Researchers' Organization, known for his study of the Craig Miller redwoods video, investigated the Snow Walker case but got little cooperation from the show's producers. They would only say that they had been given the footage by an American source who wanted the public to see it but did not want to be involved.

The truth came out after "Paranormal Borderline" was canceled. The producers themselves had created the footage, shooting it somewhere near Mammoth Mountain in California and compensating for their low-budget yeti costume by never showing a really clear view of it.

CONCLUSION: Hoax

Dave Shealy's second filming experience in the Florida Everglades, this time a videotape, from July 8th, 2000.

A frame from the Snow Walker video, not the Abominable Snowman but a bad actor in an even worse costume near Mammoth Mountain, California.

3

GALLERY OF THE MISSING

A strangely dubious collection of additions to our gallery, this; dubious, obviously, because the pictures in question are not here for us to examine and evaluate, yet strangely so because someone somewhere has obviously done so at some point.

The photos and films in this section have almost all been examined by investigators at least once. A few have been published or publicly displayed in obscure places, while others have been seen only once or twice and promptly dismissed and forgotten, their whereabouts and that of their owners presently unknown. Reasons vary as to why they do not appear here, ranging from stubborn copyright holders to an almost phantom-like elusiveness of existing prints, yet enough information remains for this brief run-through. One star indicates a single filming, two indicates more than one.

PHOTOGRAPHERS: Lennart Strand & Alden Hoover and Robert James, Jr. & Leroy Larwick
LOCATION: Near Sonora, California
DATES: February 28th, 1963, and January 6th, 1968

The uniqueness of this case (two cases actually) makes one

81

wonder why more attention has not been paid to it. It involves a truly bizarre coincidence- possibly the same creature being photographed in the same area twice, nearly five years apart, and both times by a pair of men from an overflying plane.

Strand and Hoover were flying over Confidence Ridge near Sonora when they saw a cinnamon-colored "half bear, half gorilla" standing about ten feet tall on the ground below. They took photos of the beast, but under those conditions, they turned out quite blurry. An article in the July, 1963 issue of Fate magazine stated that "their films showed nothing but rocky terrain."

The story of Larwick and James five years later appeared in the Sonora Union- Democrat. telling of a Polaroid shot snapped from a distance of about 40 yards and an altitude of 40 feet. The article stated:

"The creature was sighted about 9:30 a.m... (it is) 10-12 feet tall, with legs about half the total height. Its long arms appear to have an extra joint near the wrist. And the tall, slim figure is covered in 'brownish, matted hair.'

'The outline is sharp in the photograph, but details are shadowed. Larwick suggested it might be female because 'of some features about the chest.

"They were passing over Cherokee Ridge, south of Twin Harte, when pilot James saw something moving in the brush below.

"'T thought it was a bear, but we turned back for a closer look,' he said.

"He dipped the Cessna 150 in low and aimed it for the animal.

"At closer range, they could see it was not a bear. Larwick clicked the Polaroid camera as the small plane swooped over.

"The animal stood still during the approach, Larwick said, but 'raised its arms and fell back into the brush' as the craft passed overhead."

The men returned later on the ground and on an old logging road found footprints 20 inches long, which they also photographed. Originally, they had been en route to an air tour of Yosemite National Park, but this incident headed off their plans and is said to have caused quite a stir in the press. The men were supposedly offered large sums of money for the photo, which they were planning to keep in a safe deposit box, but nothing more seems to have materialized.

The paper did show a picture of Larwick and James, both 30 years old, looking at their creature photo- which, typically, had its backside to the camera. The article mentioned the 1963 incident briefly, though not the photos taken at the time:

"One was sighted in about the same area as the one that appeared Saturday. Pilot Lennart Strand and a passenger saw it on the ridge while on a snow survey flight."

An inquiry to the Union-Democrat in 1990 produced copies of the original article and others on some 1963 creature sightings in the area, along with a note stating, "The enclosed is all we have in our files on Big Foot. No one here recalls any photographs being made available, and due to lack of time, I am unable to track anything down."

A few more words were added by John Green, who wrote in a letter, "I think I saw the Lennart Strand photo long ago. Anyway I am sure it was just an unidentifiable blur. I don't recall seeing the Larwick photo, but I do have a note that people I talked to in Sonora had serious doubts about this report."

Though publication of the photo was said to be pending in 1968, no further information has been found in this case. With such a sensation being raised at the outset, this is most puzzling.

Now, a truly disturbing case of "small world." The name of Larwick was mentioned again in 1999 in connection to the Bigfoot subject, but in a way that no one could have predicted.

Michael Larwick, son of Leroy, grew up with a history of serious violent crimes and brushes with the law, and his only claim to fame was said to be his father's Bigfoot photo, which he would often bring up to anyone willing to listen. Then, in the spring of 1999, Michael became one of the prime suspects in the brutal kidnapping and murder of three sightseers in the Yosemite National Park area- mother and daughter Carole and Juli Sund and a teenage friend visiting from Argentina, Silvina Pelosso. Carole and Silvina's bodies were found in the trunk of a burned car near Sonora, Juli's in another location.

Larwick was arrested after a gun battle and standoff with police, but in July- five months after the Sund/Pelosso murders- a Yosemite Institute naturalist named Joie Ruth Armstrong was killed and decapitated at her home inside the park. As Larwick was in jail at the time, his guilt in the earlier crime became seriously in doubt, and he was cleared entirely three days after the new killing with the arrest of Cary Anthony Stayner, a handyman at the lodge where Carole, Juli, and Silvina had been staying. Stayner confessed to all four murders.

But even then, the wheels of synchronicity were not through turning, for Stayner too was said to be obsessed with Bigfoot and insisted he had seen one in Yosemite. It was that very subject, in fact, that he used to approach Joie Armstrong when he killed her.

Obviously, this is off on a tangent from the focus of this book, but a most dramatic one that begged to be mentioned.

PHOTOGRAPHERS: Leroy Yarborough & Jerry Oakes
LOCATION: Near Caddo, Texas
DATE: Summer, 1964

A series of creature sightings throughout northeast Texas in the 1960s produced an alleged cine film of a beast locally known as the "Caddo Critter" in Stephens County. A 1969 letter to investigator/scientist Ivan T. Sanderson from Thomas R. Adams of Paris, Texas stated, "...an obscure amateur movie which reportedly showed the creature in action was shown on WBAP-TV in Forth Worth. I remember seeing the film, and it was difficult to tell anything from viewing the t.v. although the film did not seem near as revealing as the Patterson Bigfoot film."

That may be an understatement. A 1989 inquiry to WBAP (which changed its call letters to KXAS in 1974) brought the following response:

"Unfortunately, as detailed in our broadcast of August 4th, 1964, the 'Critter' was a practical joke played by four area young people:

Leroy Yarborough, Jerry Oakes and Florence Hale of nearby Arlington, and David Phillips of Forth Worth. Yarborough and Oakes shot the film, Hale rented the gorilla suit, and Phillips wore it."

KXAS no longer had a copy of the film.

PHOTOGRAPHER: Anonymous
LOCATION: Near Nelagony, Oklahoma
DATE: 1967

Another account from the South:

In "Sasquatch: The Apes Among Us," John Green relates an account derived from an Oklahoma City-based group called the International Society for the Investigation of the Unexplained, in which an anonymous pilot made a forced landing in woods near Nelagony in northeast Oklahoma and saw a strange creature while walking out. He first spied it from a distance, thinking it to be a man and waving at it, but later saw it from only 30 feet away and described it as apelike, seven feet tall and with green glowing eyes in a large head. "He is reported to have taken a picture of it," Green writes, "but if so, I don't know what became of it."

PHOTOGRAPHER: Dave Churchill
DATE: June, 1967

Another truly remarkable story that has for some reason received only minimal attention involves a group of teenagers who claimed to have spent several nights playing a cat-and-mouse game with a number of sasquatches on the edge of a heavily populated area, heavily armed and actually shooting and wounding at least one creature. This was later investigated by Roger Patterson, fresh from his most famous experience of filming Bigfoot at Bluff Creek.

The story first came to attention when one of the youths wrote to Argosy magazine, which had just printed images from Patterson's film. The letter read:

"For several days last June, three friends and I were in constant contact with what is known on the West Coast as Sasquatch and to the rest of the world as a yeti. There was more than one of them, and we took pictures of the footprints, which ranged from nineteen to twenty-three and a half inches in length. The dimensions of the creatures are roughly from eight to ten feet tall, and the weight would be in the neighborhood of 450 pounds. I want to impress upon you that this is serious business.

"*I took pictures of this yeti* and was as close as five feet to it. The thing stalked us as much as we stalked it.

"One more startling fact is that it all took place within two miles of The Dalles, Oregon, a city with a population of 11,000, famed as the end of the Oregon Trail.

D.C."

Unfortunately, a single sentence appears to be the only information we have on the photos taken of the creatures in this case. Did Patterson or any other investigators ever see them? No one seems to know, but in the 1980 edition of "On the Track of the Sasquatch," John Green commented, "Presumably, the pictures did not amount to much, since they have never been mentioned further..."

PHOTOGRAPHER: Ron Smith
LOCATION: Cub Lake near Darrington, Washington
DATE: Summer, 1970

Smith, of Bellingham, Washington, was spending his spare time searching an area east of Darrington where two boys had reported seeing sasquatches the previous summer. He found tracks several times, and once- as told in "The Sasquatch File" by John Green- saw a creature himself and had a camera at the ready:

"Once, he said, he saw a sasquatch peering out of a bush beside a trail. He shot a color slide of it, badly out of focus, which does contain the blurred image of an ape-like face."

Green elaborated on this in a 1998 letter by saying, "The 1970s was certainly the decade for blurred pictures... The Cub lake slide I have studied at length. It had some curious bits and pieces in it but nothing identifiable. I long ago lost touch with Ron

Smith, who took it. I don't doubt his story. I recall that he loaned the slide to someone and never got it back."

PHOTOGRAPHER: Unknown
LOCATION: Idaho
DATE: 1972

Very limited information here. There is a still photo allegedly of a sasquatch taken by a man somewhere in Idaho, some time in 1972, that has been displayed in Jon Eric Beckjord's Cryptozoology Museum in Malibu, California. Beckjord called it a good shot.

PHOTOGRAPHERS: Mr. & Mrs. B.S.
LOCATION: Near Houston, British Columbia
DATE: 1972

John Green and fellow investigator Dennis Gates looked into this case involving a couple (initials used for anonymity) who had experienced some creature sightings in 1971. Then the following year, the wife was taking movies inside a neighbor's house and inadvertently captured what may have been a white-haired sasquatch through a window, walking by a creek a considerable distance away. Green stated that the film looked interesting, but that there was also a photo taken by the husband, which was supposed to show a possible creature, but "we couldn't identify anything in it."

PHOTOGRAPHERS: Anonymous
LOCATION: North Park, Allegheny County, Pennsylvania
DATE: March 28th, 1975

Two investigators from the Pennsylvania Center for UFO Research were driving on South Montour Road, hoping to see the sasquatch-type creature that had been sighted in the area. At around midnight, they saw two tall figures with red shining eyes approaching their car as if trying to circle it. The investigators took a number of photos and immediately left the area. The photos vaguely showed the red eyes.

PHOTOGRAPHER: Joe Speck
LOCATION: Samuel P. Taylor State Park, California
DATE: August, 1975

Jon Eric Beckjord reported seeing this super-8 film shot in Marin County. It was out of focus and at extreme zoom but showed a large, gray-black bipedal figure striding over some logs, partially hidden by leaves.

PHOTOGRAPHER: J.W.
LOCATION: Near Orofino, Idaho
DATE: October 24th, 1975

J.W. (initials used for anonymity) went elk hunting in the early morning near Orofino in northern Idaho, parking his pickup truck on a logging road and beginning to use an elk call. Heavy snow began to fall as time went by. Eventually, he heard something coming and got his rifle ready, but instead of an elk, a dark-colored sasquatch appeared and stood by a bush about 60 yards away. The man set the gun aside and got out his super-8 movie camera. Although filming conditions were poor in the worsening snowstorm, he managed to capture a few seconds of footage of the motionless creature, moving a few times to get different angles. It moved away as he was changing positions.

John Green says of this film, "...it is a possible. One of those that if the story is true, it is a picture of a sasquatch, and no specific reason to doubt the story." He adds, however, that its quality is too poor to be of much real value.

PHOTOGRAPHER: John Sohl

LOCATION: Citrus County, Florida
DATE: November, 1975

A group of seven young men, including Sohl, 18, was camping when they saw three creatures ("Skunk Apes," as the sasquatch is often called in Florida) around their campfire, the biggest of which was about eight feet tall. The group decided to try and photograph the creatures, and Sohl was crouched down with a camera set for medium-range as his companions searched the shadows. He thought it might have been the soft whine of the camera charging up that attracted the creature that appeared suddenly just two feet behind him. He turned to see it just as it ran past him and knocked him over with a flailing arm, and the camera went off. Had it been set for a closer range shot, it may have showed the creature clearly, but as it happened, the resulting photo showed only a dark blur.

This is probably the kind of photo one keeps forever and shows off with great pride even though it is completely useless.

PHOTOGRAPHER: Anonymous
LOCATION: Harewood Park, Maryland
DATE: November, 1975

In the Big Days Swamp area of Harewood park, three boys aged 16 and 17 reported seeing a 7 1/2 to eight-foot foul-smelling creature on three different nights. One of them photographed it, but the film was exposed. It is not clear whether this resulted in just the damage or the total erasure of the picture.

PHOTOGRAPHER: Barbara Pretula (or Pratula)
LOCATION: East Kootenay-Kimberly area, British Columbia
DATE: September, 1976

Two sightings occurred in this area, the first by Mickey McLelland, who reported seeing a tall tan-colored creature that he followed for a time down a road in his car. Next, Barbara Pretula saw what was apparently a different creature, black with a light-colored stomach and standing six to seven feet tall, behind a store she operated. She snapped a photo of it, of which John Green says, "I don't recall ever seeing this picture... an RCMP constable, who will be long gone, said it was a 'good photo though a little blurred, but police thought it was a man in a suit."

PHOTOGRAPHER: Anonymous
LOCATION: Ennis, Montana area
DATE: October, 1976

Greg Mastel, a young sasquatch enthusiast from Missoula, Montana, told John Green about a game guide who had photos of two upright eight to nine-foot figures taken from about 100 yards away. Mastel had not actually seen the pictures, however.

PHOTOGRAPHER: Anonymous
LOCATION: Ruthven, Ontario area
DATE: June 4th, 1977

A 15-year-old boy was looking out from the veranda of a house overlooking a gorge and saw a tall, black, upright creature almost hidden in some foliage. He took two photographs that seem to show a blackhead among the leaves, but no details are
apparent.

This case was investigated by Wayne King of the Michigan/Canadian Bigfoot Information Center in Caro, Michigan, who seems to consider it valid, but in a 1990 letter, King wrote, "...all of our witness supplied photography is highly classified and not available publicly or for reproduction."

PHOTOGRAPHER: Unknown
LOCATION: Silver Lake, California
DATE: August, 1977

Investigator Rich Grumley of the former California Bigfoot Organization had a case involving "blurred pictures" in connection with a
reported sighting of a seven-foot creature with long white hair in the
mountains near Silver Lake, north of Mammoth Lakes in east-central
California.

PHOTOGRAPHERS: Mr. & Mrs. Frank White
LOCATION: Mt. Baker or Lummi Reservation, Washington
DATE: October 7th, 1977

This film is rather notorious and is generally regarded as a fake by
sasquatch investigators.

The Whites had been interested in sasquatch for years, searching
various Pacific Northwest locales, and according to their story, had
gone to Mt. Baker by way of Maple Falls when their film was shot.
While having lunch Mrs. White said she thought she saw a bear, and
her husband decided to film it with a rented super-8 movie camera,
but when it entered a clearing, it turned out to be a sasquatch. The
resulting footage is 52 seconds long and shows a dark figure mean-
dering slowly through the underbrush, seemingly without purpose,
about 100 feet from the camera. Little detail is evident, but enlargements seem to show a mostly bald head. Though the creature looked
at them without apparent aggression, the couple then became fearful
and left the scene.

Frank White was very active in attracting attention to his film and
soliciting opinions on it, and he showed it at the 1978 conference held
at the University of British Columbia in Vancouver to study the
mystery of sasquatch and similar creatures. It was not well received,
and in fact, no one seems to have ever been particularly impressed
with it.

About the only book that has given more than casual mention to
the White film is 1979's "Sasquatch Apparitions" by the late psycholo-
gist Barbara Wasson, who viewed it at the UBC conference, and her
overall evaluations were not kind. In her opinion, the alleged creature
had a "droopy silhouette" and did not move naturally at all but

appeared to wander around "in oblivion like Ferdinand smelling the flowers."

(Wasson's book also mentioned Prof. Grover Krantz having endorsed the White film, but in 1992 Krantz appeared on television and stated that he thought all the alleged sasquatch films he had seen were fakes except Roger Patterson's.)

Certain aspects of the story were also unflattering, such as the Whites' incredible luck in encountering a sasquatch the day after renting a movie camera and their claim that they had been unable to relocate the film site, thereby preventing its examination.

The story finally unraveled when investigators discovered the film was not shot on Mt. Baker but on the Lummi Indian Reservation (where the Whites had searched for evidence before), and that they had rented a costume prior to the filming.

PHOTOGRAPHER: Anonymous
LOCATION: Near Tupelo, Mississippi
DATE: Fall, 1977

A motoring couple with a child reportedly took a super-8 film of a sasquatch running on or parallel to a set of railroad tracks. The film was allegedly analyzed by the Jet Propulsion Laboratory in Pasadena, California (results unknown) and was in the possession of California sasquatch investigators Barbara Ann Slate and Vince Gironda (both now deceased). Daniel Perez of the Center for Bigfoot Studies in Norwalk, California, feels the film may be genuine but admits it is hard to make out much detail.

In the December, 1998 issue of the Bigfoot Times newsletter, Perez asked Ohio investigator Don Keating what he thought of the Mississippi film. Keating replied:

"...I understand it was taken in the fall of 1977 somewhere near Tupelo, Mississippi, by a family who had been picnicking. They saw the creature on the opposite side of a set of railroad tracks. The passenger, apparently the wife, grabbed the 8mm home movie camera and began filming as they were driving. They did not stop the car because they were afraid that whatever it was would approach them and attack... All I ever saw were still photos... Reportedly, the film has been lost.

PHOTOGRAPHER: Unknown
LOCATION: Standing Rock Reservation, South Dakota
DATE: Late 1977

During the second half of 1977, a nationally publicized series of sasquatch encounters took place around the Indian community of Little Eagle, with 28 sightings from August to December indicating the presence of at least three separate creatures.

Jon Eric Beckjord of California has displayed in his Cryptozo-oology Museum what he referred to in brief correspondence as "Dart photos" from Little Eagle. Beckjord s description was of "A very spec-tral BF, looking half like a death's head. Would not care to meet that one. 200 yards, much enlarged, but ok. We computer-enhanced it. Ran on four legs, then got up and stood on two. Looked at sheriff from behind a bush, standing." I had wondered if "Dart" was supposed to be the photographer's name or if it meant something else, but then I found reference in the book "The Yeti, Bigfoot & True Giants" by Mark A. Hall to an article on the Little Eagle events in the March, 1978 issue of Argosy magazine- "A Bigfoot Sighting in South Dakota" by Sam Dart. The name is not likely to be a coincidence, but Hall's book makes no mention of Mr. Dart obtaining photos.

No other account of the Little Eagle episode (and there were a lot of them, both in print and on television) has ever mentioned this or any other filming.

PHOTOGRAPHER: Anonymous
LOCATION: Near Westfield, Massachusetts
DATE: September 10th, 1978

On February 11th, 1979, the Springfield Republican reported on a 21-year-old engineering student who had taken six fuzzy color photos of a creature he'd seen in a swamp four miles north of Cobble Mountain Reservoir five months previously. He thought it was a bear until he realized it was walking upright, and though no size estimate was given for his particular case, the article told of other sightings of a creature six to eight feet tall.

PHOTOGRAPHER: Unknown
LOCATION: Washington
DATE: 1978 (?)

A small newsletter distributed by two adolescents in Edina, Minnesota and entitled the Minnesota Bigfoot News (which actually contained all but nothing in the way of information from that state and was at least 50% reprinted material from the popular Bigfoot News of Oregon's Bigfoot Information Center in the Dalles) featured this briefest of accounts in September of 1978:

"WASHINGTON: Report of a Seattle man obtaining moving pictures of a bigfoot family. An officer of the county says that the pictures are unconvincing, and furthermore, a gorilla suit was purchased three days before the pictures were said to be taken."

My hunch is that this is most likely a convoluted account of the Frank White film of a year earlier. The Edina lads were enthusiastic, but- alas- in their youth were sometimes not very accurate.

PHOTOGRAPHER: Marion Schubert
LOCATION: California (?)
DATE: 1978

Another display from Beckjord's Cryptozoology Museum. Unfortunately, no further detail has been provided on this photo except by John Green, who said in a 1998 letter, "Regarding Marion Schubert, my failing memory tells me that this was the woman that Beckjord spent a great deal of time with quite a few years ago, regarding repeated incidents at a campground in, I think, California. It seems to me that there was a lot more reported than I was prepared to accept...

I suppose, though, that the picture was probably burned up when he lost most of his other stuff."

(Beckjord once lost his home in one of the raging fires that plague southern California from time to time, and most of the Bigfoot material he had at that time was destroyed.)

PHOTOGRAPHER: Unknown
LOCATION: Mt. Rainier, Washington
DATE: 1979

Michigan's Wayne King saw some poor-quality photos taken on Mt. Rainier, but no further information is available.

PHOTOGRAPHER: Unknown
LOCATION: South-Central Canada
DATE: Late 1970s (?)

This account comes from an acquaintance, C.J. of Moorhead, Minnesota, who recalls once knowing a man who used to take annual canoe trips from Canada back down to the U.S. (the most likely route would be the Boundary Waters Canoe Area between Minnesota and Ontario). On one such outing, the man said, while at a campsite in Canada, he had heard, then seen a sasquatch and photographed it in the darkness. C.J. remembers seeing the picture and says it was of the typical "looming silhouette" type, but as it was several years ago, further details have escaped him, including the man's name and present whereabouts.

PHOTOGRAPHER: Unknown
LOCATION: Near Beacon Rock, Washington
DATE: 1982

This brief report appears in issue #20 of The Track Record. August 1992:

"One last item for Vane (Brouley). Ten years ago, he stopped to pick up a fellow on the road carrying a five-gallon gas can. The can he found out was a sham, hinged, the hitcher used it as a suitcase... get more rides that way. The fellow had with him, though, a stack of photos of Bigfoot. He claimed to have run across a whole family of them on Woodward Creek, near Beacon Rock, Wa., and was anxious to have people see his photos. Vane skeptically looked at several of the photos, but said he could only see an outline of something with red eyes from the flashbulbs."

PHOTOGRAPHER: Unknown
LOCATION: Near McCarthur, Ohio
DATE: May, 1988

Sasquatch hunters Bob Gardiner and Mike Claar guided a number of media reporters and cameramen into the Experimental Forest in southern Ohio, where there had been recent creature sightings. The group found tracks and heard mysterious howling at night. Walkie-talkies began to malfunction, and Gardiner said electronic gear often failed when sasquatch was nearby.

The camera crew managed to zoom in on and film a glowing eye about a hundred yards from their camp.

PHOTOGRAPHER: Anonymous
LOCATION: Derry Township, Pennsylvania
DATE: June 29th, 1988

A rural family was experiencing strange events, including the finding of 16-inch footprints and damage to a fence and some floodlights that were six feet off the ground. Their animals were also acting strangely. After three days, at 7:30 a.m., they saw a seven or eight-foot creature with stringy, grayish-brown hair walking near where some horses were kept.

The case was investigated by Stan Gordon of the Pennsylvania Association for the Study of the Unexplained. An article in the Latrobe Bulletin on July 14th stated, "Photos of the creature taken by the family did not turn out, a disappointed Gordon added, due to a problem with the camera." It does not specify whether something indistinguishable was actually down on film or if the film was totally ruined.

PHOTOGRAPHERS: Anonymous
LOCATION: Patapsco Valley State Park, Maryland
DATE: 1988

A paranormal research group called Center Force claimed to have filmed sasquatches a number of times in this park near Baltimore, including one videotape shot by a man sitting in a truck when a creature crossed the road in front of him.

Writer Mark Opsasnick, who investigated sasquatch reports throughout Maryland for several years and assembled an incredibly huge collection of reports before concluding that the creature was not physically real but only a cultural phenomenon, said of the incident, "The tape is very blurry. You see a dark black form, and it's in view for one or two seconds. There's no possible way I could conclude that that was Bigfoot."

Opsasnick said the Center Force group was practically a cult and warned against taking any of their claims seriously. I can neither confirm nor deny that allegation.

(As a matter of interest, Patapsco Valley State Park was seen by millions of moviegoers in 1999 as one of the locations where "The Blair Witch Project" was filmed.)

PHOTOGRAPHER: Betty Parks
LOCATION: Coshocton County, Ohio
DATE: November 1st, 1988

The Cleveland Plain Dealer told this story on January 9th, 1989:
"...Betty Parks of Eaton, near Dayton, had photographic proof that Bigfoot had
visited.

"In the darkness at Muddy Creek Lane on November 1st, Parks had fired a few frames with her small 35mm camera at a rustling noise coming from behind a patch of roadside weeds. Parks had one of the snapshots enlarged to show the face of a Bigfoot poking through the weeds.

"Unfortunately, to those with only a little less imagination, the face looked much like the other brown clumps of faded goldenrod that abundantly grow along the roadside."

Parks was with a friend, Richard Myers, staking out the area after an incident earlier that day in which something unseen but which made bipedal-sounding footfalls had thrown a rotten log in their direction. During the nocturnal stakeout, piercing yells were heard, and then a crashing noise in the weeds just a few yards from the car in which the two sat. Eyes were seen reflecting a flashlight beam an instant before the picture was taken.

Don Keating, a noted sasquatch investigator from Newcomerstown, Ohio, was asked his opinion of the Parks photo in an interview in issue #4 of The Sasquatch Report newsletter, July 1990. His response:

"The photo leaves a lot to the imagination. One person looks at it and says it is a young Bigfoot creature. However, another person looks at it and says it is nothing more than the goldenrod, a type of weed. I personally think it could be a young Bigfoot-type creature."

PHOTOGRAPHER: Don Keating
LOCATION: Coshocton County, Ohio
DATE: 1991-1992

Don Keating himself has also been involved in filming what may have been the eastern Ohio sasquatch, and on more than one occasion.

On the evening of September 15th, 1991, a controversial piece of footage was captured in Christian Chapel Cemetery near Coshocton. As in the Parks case, Keating and associate Richard Mortz had heard strange noises in the woods near the cemetery earlier in the day and had returned with a camcorder and 500,000 candlepower floodlight. Heavy breathing noises were then heard in the cemetery, and a sweep of the area was made with the light and camera, but nothing unusual was seen at the time. When the tape was viewed later, however, what appeared to be a black creature of some kind was stooped over beside a gravestone. Though many believed a sasquatch had been filmed that evening, some skeptical investigators dismissed it as only a shadow.

The debate ended in September of 1992 when Keating viewed the tape in slow motion. It turned out to be neither a sasquatch nor a shadow exactly but what he called "a unique optical illusion" caused by the floodlight. In slow motion, the creature could be seen materializing out of nothing beside the gravestone.

Three months later, on December 22nd, he videotaped an incident that he described in a letter:

"Myself and a local resident of Coshocton took to the hills to look around for any signs of the creature being in the area. We had a set of walkie-talkies and once we got to a certain point, decided to go in two different directions. As I got to an area where there is a very large open field, I spotted what I thought was the other man. So, I decided to videotape him and see how good it would look. After all, he was between 250 and 350 yards from me. This was at 5:04 p.m. Little did I know that the other man (I'll call him

Jack), was around a bend along the side of the woods line watching something also, which wasn't me! He described it as being between 7 and 7 1/2 feet tall; dark in color with black being the main color but patches of brown; barrel-chested, and it had long arms which hung down to its knees. He could see it walking very plainly, and noted that the arms didn't really move that much as it was walking.

"Remember I said I thought I was videotaping Jack in the middle of the open field? Well, it turns out it MAY not have been him. What I got on tape was almost the exact same thing he reported seeing. What I have on videotape is a bi-pedal individual walking away from me, dark in color, with arms that hang down to close to the knees. It appears to be very bulky."

Another video followed on August 2nd, 1992, this time of what appeared to be a white creature, but it only appears on the tape for a few seconds. This clip was featured on a t.v. program on the Learning Channel on February 28th, 2000.

PHOTOGRAPHER: Unknown
LOCATION: Oregon
DATE: Fall, 1993 (?)

This mention in the Bigfoot Co-Op. very brief, came in October, 1993:

"New Report- Sighting of a Bigfoot in Oregon with clear photographs. This information is from a reliable source who is not involved in Bigfoot research. Hopefully, photos will be on their way to the Co-Op."

There was never any further mention.

PHOTOGRAPHER: Unknown
LOCATION: Coon Rapids, Minnesota
DATE: Summer of Fall, 1995 (?)

I heard personally from some acquaintances that someone in the Coon Rapids area north of Minneapolis had supposedly achieved clear videotape of a sasquatch. Much as I would like this to be true, however (as it would be the only example of such photography in my home state), I do not trust this source and doubt that such a video actually exists.

PHOTOGRAPHER: Anonymous
LOCATION: Southern Alaska
DATE: January, 1997

Jon Eric Beckjord was contacted by an Alaska man who had an unusual experience while ice fishing on a small frozen lake. Between one and two p.m., he heard a "whoomp" sound and the crashing of brush on the opposite shore, then thought he saw a bear moving through the trees. A second "whoomp" then sounded, this time behind him, and though he was starting to become nervous, he took out his video camera and began filming what happened next out on the snow-covered ice.

The video shows a tall, erect, brown or black figure moving on to the ice a considerable distance away and walking from right to left toward a small island, covering a distance of 80-90 yards through fairly deep snow that seems to cause a steady but shuffling sort of walk. The body seems very muscular, with thick bunches of hair on the head and shoulders and on the legs, which swings back and forth with each step. It pauses several times and at one point seems to move toward the fisherman, but then continues on to the island, where it is briefly lost to view behind a rise. When it reappears, it turns and goes back along the same route, back on to the ice and back to where it had first appeared, traveling this time without pause until it disappears into the woods.

The fisherman was afraid to go out and look for tracks because of the sounds he had heard behind him, and locked himself in his truck for 45 minutes before finally leaving the area.

The case seemed promising until the fisherman made comparison videos later to try and make sense of what he had seen. In the April, 1998 issue of the Bigfoot Co-Op, Beckjord reported on the results of the tests:

"Comparison videos made by the witness now show us that the original object was less than 6 feet tall and could, in theory, have had snowmobile pants unzipped at the ankles, wearing perhaps a parka with a hood up. Further testing is being done. Anything filmed at 1,000 feet is difficult. However, the assistant of the witness during the comparison filming felt watched and felt that something was in the brush near him during that filming. Frame-grabbing of the video shows in one frame a face that looks like 'YOSEMITE SAM' or an owl-like demon typeface. At such a distance, who can know for sure? Overall odds are so far that Bigfoot is not involved."

PHOTOGRAPHER: Anonymous
LOCATION: Near Breckenridge Mountain, California
DATE: September 4th, 2000

A Bakersfield man reported to Daniel Perez of the Center for Bigfoot Studies that his wife had captured a couple of seconds of videotape of a possible sasquatch while they were out four-wheeling over the Labor Day weekend. Shot from a moving vehicle at 3:10 p.m., the footage shows a dark upright figure with arms longer than a man's moving from a clearing into some woods. As this book was being completed, this case was still under investigation by Mr. Perez.

PHOTOGRAPHER: Steve Piper
LOCATION: Brindabella ranges, Australia
DATE: September 8th, 2000

The Associated Press released the following report dealing with the yowie, the little-known Australian version of Bigfoot:

"A Canberra bushwalker has footage of a large unidentified creature that he believes could be a yowie.

"Amateur cameraman Steve Piper captured the mystery animal while filming for a video clip in the Brindabella ranges, south of Canberra.

"He says he was filming what he thought was a large kangaroo in a gully, when he realized it was far too big to be a kangaroo.

"The bewildered Mr. Piper has delivered the footage to a research group investigating possible yowie sightings. The footage has been touted as the best of its kind since an alleged Bigfoot sighting at Bluff Creek in the United States in 1968.

"A researcher says it is the most conclusive evidence to date that a Bigfoot creature may be roaming the Australian wilderness.

"Further investigations will now be carried out in the Brindabel-las, where two sightings have been reported in the past century."

Here the writer has mistakenly placed the Patterson film a year past its actual date. As for Piper's film, it is eight to ten seconds long and shows the creature moving from left to right with a bad limp in its right leg, about 50 yards from the camera.

Dean Harrison, a noted yowie investigator in Australia, has expressed some doubt about the film but does not appear to be entirely convinced it is a hoax, saying, "I'm going to have to fence-sit this one."

PHOTOGRAPHER: Jon Eric Beckjord
LOCATION: California Sierras
DATE: Various, unknown

In addition to the people showcased in his Cryptozoology Museum and the others he has investigated, Mr. Beckjord has himself produced alleged evidence of the sasquatch on film. In fact, he has a whole series of photos he claims to have taken in the Sierra Mountains. One of these, reportedly of a six to seven-foot female creature in a squatting position, appeared in The Skeptical Enquirer.

In a brief response to an inquiry about his sasquatch photos, Beckjord wrote, "Have five good ones, including one showing half a BF. There is no other half."

In the August 2000 issue of the Bigfoot, Co-Op Beckjord had an ad for tee shirts he has for sale depicting various sasquatch photos, including two frames from the Patterson film and three of his own Sierra shots. In addition to the "Half-Bigfoot" shot, he also listed "Big Mama Sierra Bigfoot" and "Dual-face paranormal Sierra Bigfoot."

Comments like this- alluding to Beckjord's intangible, inter-dimensional theories on the creatures' origins- have brought him little respect or attention from many investigators. John Green, however, stated in a letter, "I do not consider him unreliable at all. I don't agree with his theories, I don't see the same things he sees in pictures, and I know he has a lot of people fed up with him, but I have full confidence in his sincerity and thoroughness as an investigator."

PHOTOGRAPHER: Anonymous
LOCATION: East Liberty, Ohio
DATE: Unknown

A minister with an interest in the sasquatch who lives about 30 miles northwest of Columbus was told this story.

It was the birthday of an East Liberty man, and his family had gathered in his home, having bought him an easy chair. That evening his mother asked the man to sit in his new chair so she could take a picture of him in it. When she looked through the camera, she saw a pair of eyes looking through the window behind her son, and she snapped the picture. Although the glare from the glass distorted it, the photo reportedly showed a hazy image of a sasquatch looking in. Afterward, the creature roamed about the property often, and the family came to think of it almost like a pet.

PHOTOGRAPHER: Anonymous
LOCATION: Ohio
DATE: Unknown

Another Ohio case: As this book was being completed, investigator Tim Olson of Arcata, California, reported that he was in contact with a Milwaukee, Wisconsin woman whose mother had three photos of a sasquatch taken in Ohio. Few details were available, but Tim planned to look into this further.

PHOTOGRAPHER: R. Ravzhir
LOCATION: Mongolia
DATE: Unknown

We close this section of the gallery with another foreign report, involving one of the sasquatch's Asian counterparts this time. The

March 20th, 1988 edition of Tokyo, Japan's Mainichi Daily News contained the following brief:

"A Mongolian adventurer claims he made plaster molds of an abominable snowman's footprints *and photographed the creature sitting on a rock*, a Soviet newspaper reported.

"...R. Ravzhir spent 1,340 days searching for the beast Mongolians call 'yeti' or 'almas.' He succeeded in seeing from a distance the snowman three times and more than 30 times photographed his footprints and gathered dozens of eyewitness accounts about the almas, the newspaper said."

4

SPECIAL CASES

A few more items still remain, hanging far, far back in their own dimly-lit corner of the Beastly Gallery.

Why are these special cases? In part because of certain dubious aspects of the photographers' stories, but even more so in many of these cases, it is because of the extreme... well, *goofiness* of the pictures themselves. They are so blatantly outrageous that nearly everyone in or out of the sasquatch field would agree that there is no way in Heaven or Earth they could be real.

Yes, "nearly everyone." Amazing as it may seem, these photos and films have been presented as genuine evidence for the existence of sasquatch, and somehow there have been those who have accepted them.

This is America, of course, land of the free where we must steadfastly defend the right of the people to believe whatever they wish, and I must state for the record that I am only saying that I and many others believe these cases to be hoaxes (as we are also free to do). Anyone else is free to believe whatever they like, and to cite established facts as foundation for their beliefs. To wit:

PAUL FREEMAN

Mr. Freeman is perhaps the most unique of the special cases, for he has been involved with a great variety of alleged sasquatch evidence, some of which has caused a genuine stir in scientific circles. Most of the story is outside the scope of this book, so a general rundown will suffice (especially since many who follow the sasquatch field will already be familiar with it).

Freeman claimed that on June 10th, 1982, while patrolling the Mill Creek Watershed in southeast Washington's Blue Mountains as part of his job with the Forest Service, he encountered a huge sasquatch at very close range. Just another sighting, one might say, but it was the footprints found soon afterward that thrust the case into the spotlight. They contained dermal ridges, the foot's equivalent of fingerprints, and noted sasquatch expert and anthropologist Dr. Grover Krantz of Washington State University- one of the very few scientists to devote serious attention to the subject- called them the most convincing tracks ever found, on par with the Patterson film as evidence. In his 1992 book "Big Footprints: A Scientific Inquiry into the Reality of Sasquatch," Krantz told of showing casts of the Freeman tracks to a variety of experts, including law enforcement personnel, none of whom could see how they could have been faked. (Meanwhile, however, they had been pronounced fake by Joel Hardin, a tracking expert for the U.S. Border Patrol who had examined the actual tracks at the scene, though in his book Krantz convincingly refuted most every one of Hardin's points of contention.)

The story might have ended there, but it was only the beginning. What followed over the next several years was a seemingly endless parade of evidence- more sightings, more tracks, handprints, hair samples, even photographic events- but rarely, it seemed, unless Paul Freeman or those close to him were around. Many investigators, some of whom had labeled even the original tracks as fake, were now convinced beyond doubt that the Blue Mountains Bigfoot and Paul Freeman were one and the same entity. Freeman was no longer with the Forest Service and claimed his frequent discoveries were

due to his many hours spent in the mountains tirelessly searching for evidence on his own time.

Vance Orchard, a journalist for the Walla Walla Union-Bulletin, author of the book "Bigfoot of the Blues" and a full supporter of Freeman, has chronicled a long history of tracks and sightings in the area going back several decades, and even John Green has stated (though not endorsing Freeman) that it's quite likely the sasquatch does dwell there. Krantz continues to stand by the case, but investigators such as veteran Rene Dahinden have been very outspoken in denouncing it in none-too-subtle terms as a total sham.

The first creature photos to come to public attention in the Blue Mountains saga were taken (according to Freeman) on the morning of October 5th, 1988. He said he and his son Duane were searching near the border of the watershed when a dark-colored creature 7 1/2 feet tall and weighing from 500 to 700 pounds with grayish facial hair and extremely long arms emerged from the trees about 150 yards away. "It must have smelled us or something," Freeman said, "because the way it was headed, it should have come closer than that." In any case, he began filming with an old-fashioned movie camera, and Duane snapped pictures with a 35mm camera. Somehow the cine film did not turn out, but three still photos of Duane's appeared two days later on page one of the Union-Bulletin. They were vague, showing a typical dark manlike figure moving away from the camera.

"These pictures are great," Freeman commented. "I know that people have said all along, 'He's lying. There's nothing there.' But I know what I saw. I know what my son took pictures of."

According to other sources, there appears to have been another set of photos taken by Freeman himself somewhat earlier than this, some time in 1987, but they have received little if any public attention. They were sent to Oregon-based investigator Peter Byrne (inactive at that time, but later of the well-funded Bigfoot Research Project), who said he was unimpressed and sent them back. Jon Eric Beckjord did likewise, citing extreme range as the problem, but said they were Not fake, just too small. Later Beckjord was quite active in promoting the '88 photos and did an in-depth analysis of them for the Bigfoot Co-Op. which appeared in their April 1989 issue. To paraphrase:

"A tentative analysis of the 'back visible' Bigfoot photo by Duane Freeman, using a cropped print from the original negative offers the following subjection revision:

"Black figure, bipedal, appears to be standing, not walking, between two trees, facing away from camera.

"...Left-arm, extended, would go below buttocks but not as far as knee.

"Neck appears short or non-existent.

"...Head shows a white area on the right side (side of right eye and cheek).

"Same portion shows a prognathous (jaw-jutting) aspect in outline. It is not a flat
    face.

"A round eye-ball-like object is visible under magnification, in white-blue form...

"...Head appears flat-to-rounded on top with an area of either dense hair or muscle on the rear area.

"Hand on left seems flat with fingers, if any, held together straight. No thumb visible and no obvious wrist...

"Feet visible, obscured by either a) whitish disc about 2-3 feet wide at ankle level, or b) cloud of whitish dust from walking.

"To this viewer, there is a straw-colored 'star' in same shape as a sheriffs badge that is transparent and covers rear or right leg and open area next to leg on right, extending from waist to ankles. This could, of course, be a pattern of tall grass.

"Note- There is some resemblance between Charles Edson photo from No. Calif, and the side view of this creature's face.

"At this time, nothing to indicate a hoax. More data and study are needed."

(Author's note: I was unsuccessful in my attempts to see these photos. Beckjord, apparently acting as agent for the Freemans, became very protective of them even though they had already appeared in the newspaper. At one point during correspondence with Beckjord, he sent me a news clipping about himself, featuring a picture of him displaying the Freeman photos- which he had crossed out with a black marker.)

There was still more to come. In the late morning of April 14th, 1992, Freeman said that while in the mountains to pick mushrooms (but always alert for signs of Bigfoot), he was driving ten miles above Five Points close to the watershed boundary when he spotted a creature- apparently the same one from his son's photos- in some brush below the road about 30 yards away. He grabbed a Sony camcorder he now carried and hurriedly got out of his truck, thinking the creature would cross the road directly ahead of him, but he made the mistake of slamming the door and apparently frightened it off in the opposite direction. He ran up the road trying to get another view of it and managed to film it briefly at a distance of about 70 yards when it finally crossed the road. After it had disappeared, he trailed it for half a mile and shot 20 minutes of footage of its tracks, but the creature itself was only on the tape for 15 seconds, and as he had forgotten to zoom in, it only appeared one inch high on screen.

"You have to look at it two or three times until you see it," Freeman stated. (In the book "Sasquatch/Bigfoot: The Search for North America's Incredible Creature" by Don Hunter and Rene Dahinden, the skeptical Dahinden responds to that statement with a simple "At least," eloquently summing up the general consensus among investigators as only he can.)

More than enough waves had been made at that point to insure Paul Freeman a permanent spot in the "Who's Who" of sasquatch history, but his most amazing story of all came into being just four months later. It is best known for having been featured on the October 29th, 1992, broadcast of the t.v. tabloid show "Hard Copy," which was also reporting on recent well-documented creature sightings on a Nez Perce reservation near Lapway, Idaho. The show portrayed the two stories as if they were related when in fact, they had nothing whatsoever to do with each other, and suggested that they had begun to interview Freeman without first having known of his new video, that he had hesitantly brought out his "private tape" after production was well underway. This is almost certainly a case of dramatic license. (And what a surprise- Freeman was able to take the "Hard Copy" crew out and discover brand new tracks on their first day filming.)

A frame from Paul Freeman's Deduct Spring video of August 20th, 1992. This fails to capture the impression of the full moving video and the unnatural movements of the alleged creature.

The new tape in question, Freeman, claimed- showcased under the t.v. headline "The New Bigfoot Video"- was shot on the morning of August 20th, 1992, at a pond near Deduct Spring, 30 miles from Walla Walla, regarded by him as a popular watering hole for Bigfoot creatures where he sometimes found tracks. Sure enough, there were new tracks in the mud beside the pond on this morning with water still in them. "I said 'Jiminy Christmas,'" he quipped on the show, "'one's already been here and must have just run out of here.'"

He filmed the tracks and began following them toward the nearby woods. His voice on the tape narrates what happened next: "I hear the brush poppin' and stuff... Hoa, there he goes!"

And a hairy form strides into view from right to left. This one is not merely an inch high, not just a vague shape in a still photo, but a creature Freeman claims was possibly eight feet tall with thick black hair and a muscular body at fairly close range, although still just a little on the blurry side when enlarged for a closer look at details. It glances toward the camera with light gray facial features somewhat apparent but continues to walk through the underbrush in profile. It looks, in fact, much like the subject of Freeman's previous filmings. Could he actually be encountering the exact same individual over and over?

"Oh God," Freeman whispers with great emotion, "there's two of 'em, I guess."

The camera somehow failed to capture it, but a second, somewhat smaller creature then appeared and came straight toward him, coming close enough for him to make out a swollen deformity of some kind on the side of its face. It snarled at him before turning away and disappearing into the forest along with its larger companion, but he disregarded the warning and followed.

But the filming was over. He suddenly heard the creatures approaching with a torrent of angry noises. "They scream," he said, "just like a cougar screaming, but man, it makes the ground shake." Afraid now for his life, he hid in a cavity created by the roots of a fallen tree, trembling with fear until the creatures went away. "I was like a little five-year-old," he admitted. "I was crying, and I asked the Man Upstairs, you know, if you let me get out of here alive, I'll never bother these critters again, and I'm not going to."

And thus ended Paul Freeman's quest for sasquatch, at least on an active level, and in grand style. So was this video his ultimate achievement? Perhaps, but a close look at it also seems to summarize the character of his entire decade-long saga. The alleged creature in the Deduct Spring footage is clearly shown to be continually glancing down at its feet as it negotiates the underbrush as if unsure of its footing, hardly what one would expect in a natural walk for a wild creature but making more sense for a man in a bulky costume. Given that such a costume might exist, then, and considering its resemblance to the figure in the earlier filmings as well, the logic is clear. As they stand, these cases are really no worse than most other likely hoax films (actually, they are much better than some we will look at next), but in this Special Case of the Beastly Gallery, it is not the product itself so much as the whole set of circumstances surrounding it that brings on such suspicion and downright cynicism.

Did Paul Freeman really see a sasquatch in the Mill Creek Watershed in 1982? It is possible. The "dermal ridge" tracks, though attacked by Freeman's critics, did stand up

to expert scientific study, and none of the people who call them fake have been able to explain exactly how it might have been convincingly done.

Has Paul Freeman really been lucky enough to have numerous other sightings, to find thousands of footprints virtually everywhere he looks, and to have four separate photographic encounters? No, it must be seriously doubted.

We may be dealing here with a case of embellishment gone wild. A person doesn't feel his original experience is convincing enough, so it must be bolstered by more and more. In such a case, the hoaxer would probably feel that he is actually doing a good thing, that since the creature really does exist, it doesn't matter if the evidence is real as long as it makes people believe. Very few investigators seem to accept this scenario. To most, it is either all real or all fake, no in-between, but some of their reasoning in this case must be viewed in perspective.

The negative report of expert tracker Joel Hardin on the original Freeman tracks is often cited, as well as the statements of the local Forest Service agents who say that with their people out in the field day after day, it's quite suspicious that only a few people ever report seeing anything. But why should sasquatch hunters suddenly use such statements in their favor in this particular case when such authorities have always said such things to dismiss the very existence of sasquatch? It has also been brought to light that Freeman was known to have had a lot of interest in the creature well before his first sighting report, but as stated before, this does not automatically rule out the chance of ever encountering one. If so, then all sasquatch hunters who hunt with a camera instead of a gun might as well give up, as they will never be believed. Roger Patterson is the prime example.

Speaking of Patterson, "Hard Copy" quite incorrectly spoke of a "haunting similarity" between his 1967 film and Freeman's video, and made such blatantly unforgivable mistakes as calling him "John" instead of "Roger" and placing his filming a year later in 1968, but they also featured a brief clip of Dr. Grover Krantz stating, "I haven't seen another movie on film that compares to (Patterson's), and quite frankly I don't think any of the ones I have seen are even real, I think they're all faked. Patterson's is real." One must assume that he is including the various Freeman photos and films in this assessment. Krantz has championed the dermal ridge tracks and has been called gullible for it by some, but he has shown that he is not a man who falls for just anything.

(Incidentally, on the error in Patterson's name- There was actually a famous adventurer named John Patterson once, a British Colonel and engineer who became legendary for killing two seemingly unstoppable man-eating lions that had been feeding on the members of a railroad crew at Tsavo in Africa in 1898. He was portrayed by actor Val Kilmer in the recent film "The Ghost and the Darkness." One must wonder how the Patterson of old would feel being confused with a Bigfoot hunter.)

These are my own thoughts and opinions on what is, through it all, a quite complex case. They may be dead-on or hopelessly off the mark, for I have never been to the Blue Mountains and received no reply in my attempt to contact Paul Freeman.

But let's not overlook "Hard Copy"'s final tabloid-minded comment on the case, which sums up its overall character so very well:

"Some cynics still point to the fact that you never see Bigfoot and Howard Stem in the same room at the same time."

LYLE VANN

We move on now to those exhibits in the Beastly gallery that are so little- respected not only for the stories that go with them but also for their very appearance.

Lyle Vann is the director of the Arizona Bigfoot Center in Paulden and has claimed many encounters with sasquatch in both the central and northern parts of that state and in southern California. Multiple sightings alone are usually enough to generate strong suspicion among other investigators, but Vann's theories on the nature of the creatures are the main strike against him.

Vann states quite emphatically that sasquatches are controlled by alien beings who use them for mining gold and silver from the Earth's crust. "Their world is inside our world," he says, meaning that both races live below ground. The foul odor sometimes reported, he explains, is due to sulfur in the ground adhering to the creatures' hair. He adds that the aliens use them because they are strong but gentle, and says, "Bigfoot is very humanlike... Some of the big bulls are very identifiable individuals. I saw one with a silver collar, another with a cape."

As evidence, Vann offers numerous photographs he has taken of sasquatches, aliens, and flying saucers. UFO photos are a field unto themselves and are outside the scope of this book, but let's look at a few of the others.

One photo that blends both phenomena was printed in the April 1993 issue of the Bigfoot Co-Op with an accompanying article by Vann explaining how he had taken it in California's Angeles National Forest on January 6th, 1981. While sitting by a pond where he had had a previous creature sighting, he suddenly heard a loud bang that sounded like a metal door slamming shut. Then, not far away, he saw what was apparently a landed UFO through the trees and not just one but four sasquatches rapidly approaching him. He snapped one quick photo and then made a hasty retreat, but seemed quite pleased with the result.

Co-Op editor Connie Cameron included a disclaimer with the photo: "The picture on the following page is printed for your infor- mation. I have told Lyle Vann that I cannot make out either the UFO or the Bigfoots. He has drawn arrows and circles to indicate these things."

This note was necessary because the photo is, in fact, to all appearances, of an empty forest. (I decided not to go to the effort of reproducing it here as all it shows is a tangle of brush that is very tedious to draw.)

The previous year on October 21st, 1980, Vann had produced another southern California picture, this one featuring himself allegedly scraping what he believed to be dried sasquatch blood from a rock to have tested. Standing 35 to 40 yards behind him on the opposite bank, he says, is a large male creature dark in color and about eight feet tall. Again, it takes considerable imagination to see any trace of said creature in this photo. (Also, who took this shot? If Vann set up the camera to go off automatically, the premise of his not being aware of the creature behind him would seem to be contradicted.)

From October 21st, 1980- Vann scrapes a blood sample from a rock while in the background stands... well, apparently an invisible sasquatch. Photos by Lyle Vann.

Spring, 1987. This is it- the worst picture in the entire book. Vann claimed it showed three sasquatches and two bears. Photos by Lyle Vann.

From April 17th, 1989- Lyle Vann's shot of sasquatches scaling a cliff, part of a series of photos he says he took while viewing an entire gathering of weird creatures of all kinds.

Another shot printed in the Bigfoot Co-Op in its June 1990 issue and credited to the spring of 1987 in northern Arizona receives the prize for the absolute worst photo in the entire Beastly Gallery, quite a distinction. Vann claimed it showed another large male sasquatch cuddling a baby bear cub as an adult bear sat calmly in the background with a female creature, which in turn held a young one. A regular forest love-in, it seems. Vann wrote that he was sharing this picture to show gun-toting hunters how gentle and loving sasquatch is, and described the 8 1/2 to nine-foot male creature in great anatomical detail, which readers were apparently supposed to be able to see in the picture. (He had even measured its stooped-over height at exactly seven feet two inches.) Once again, editor Cameron added a note: "The color photo is not very clear and does not copy well, but we will try to share it with you."

Surely this must be a massive understatement. Surely the original photo shows something more. For what is shown in the Co-Op looks a bit like tree bark photographed from one inch away. That, or a psychiatrist's inkblot.

(It should be noted that Vann's story in this case also demonstrates a great lack of knowledge about the behavior of bears.)

A final shot of Vann's we'll look at here, again from northern Arizona, is from April 17th, 1989, and supposedly shows a huge 11-foot male creature offering a hand to a ten-foot female carrying a baby, to help them in scaling a rocky ledge. The creatures are just dark shapes, and on an individual basis, the photo is quite inconclusive. Strange, that, since Vann claims it is just one of many photos he took that day showing an entire conglomeration of creatures including bizarre homed aliens, an attractive female Bigfoot with a ring on one finger and sticks in her hair acting as barrettes, and a big male with a severed alien head slung over his shoulder from combat in a war that was going on with another alien race. This day changed his life forever, Vann says, and adds that the world may not be ready to see all the pictures he has taken. If they are no more impressive than the ones he has released, however, I have a hunch we can handle it.

These are only some of Lyle Vann's bizarre photos. He says he keeps the exact locations of each encounter confidential to discourage hunters with guns from finding the creatures, but such concealments do little for his stories' credibility. Nor, obviously, do the stories themselves.

RAY WALLACE

In the 1995 book "Where Bigfoot Walks: Crossing the Dark Divide" by noted naturalist Robert Michael Pyle, he describes his first contact with Ray Wallace, who wrote to him after learning of his interest in sasquatch. Very matter-of-factly, Pyle comments, "He enclosed a couple of snapshots of someone in a gorilla suit."

That is as good an introduction as any to Mr. Wallace, a fixture in the Bigfoot field for decades and one of the most amusing characters it has ever seen.

Wallace was born in 1917 in Missouri, but in only two years, his family moved west, where young Ray befriended the Indians living along Washington's Cowlitz River and would often play hooky from school to spend time with them. They taught him the art of animal tracking and other wilderness skills, and when he reached adulthood, he

began to make his living in various ways throughout the rugged terrain of the Pacific Northwest. Over the years, he has operated a free zoo, dealt in oil and precious minerals, worked in logging, and most prominently served as a contractor in road building projects into very wild country. It was as a result of this latter career that his association with sasquatch began.

Wallace was in charge of the logging road being built into the Bluff Creek wilderness of northern California in 1958 that ended up introducing the name "Bigfoot" to the world after giant footprints appeared repeatedly around the workers' heavy equipment and large barrels of fuel were carried away from the camp and tossed around like toys. He was reportedly none too happy about the disruption to his business and hired hunters to come in and do away with the creature. Needless to say, they failed, but eventually, the road did get built, and everyone concerned went their ways. The Bluff Creek region has been famous ever since as Bigfoot Country, immortalized by Roger Patterson's 1967 film.

But just after the flurry of excitement generated by the Patterson film, in November of 1970, Ray Wallace announced that he also had film footage of Bigfoot- 15,000 feet of it in fact- taken around the time of the road project and showing a dark creature ten feet tall and weighing a thousand pounds. Its wrists were eight inches thick, its fingers eight inches long, and topped by "ivory-looking claws" 1 1/2 inches long and 1/4 inch thick. Few, if any, have ever taken this footage seriously, nor any of the many photographs and other evidence Wallace has come out with over the years. In fact, as he has aged, he has taken a position not as a respected local historian and expert on sasquatch, but as a respected teller of tall tales who claims to be an expert, and most who hear his stories- laced as they are with "dawg-gones" and other colorful speech- are content to let him insist all he wants that he speaks the absolute truth.

Wallace's penchant for storytelling is not exactly a recent thing. Back in 1960, when Texas millionaire Tom Slick was sponsoring an organized hunt for Bigfoot in northern California, Wallace told him he had a creature in captivity and offered to show it to him for the right price. After some unsuccessful negotiating, the captive beast was said to have grown ill and been released.

Then there is the country music record he helped produce several decades back, featuring a song about Bigfoot interwoven with piercing shrieks Wallace says he recorded from a creature he had trapped in a deep hole. The picture on the jacket, he says, was taken by a Forest Service employee and shows a sasquatch sharing a meal with a cougar. It is a classic Ray Wallace creature- someone in a comical black shaggy costume with a high rounded head and large white claws visible on the hand that is extended to the cougar. He says it is saying "Zuki zuki" to the big cat, a gesture of friendship. (A cute little tale, but one can't help but notice how the cougar is simply staring straight ahead with a blank look on its face. Think taxidermy.)

When it comes to the Patterson film, Wallace says, "I know just which Yakima Indian was in that monkey suit." But his own films and photos appear to be quite numerous. I have personally seen four- one of a creature sitting on a log supposedly in the Mt. St. Helens area, a very vague shot of something crouched down in a clearing of high grass, another of a creature crouched beside a pond apparently feeding on something, and the famous cougar photo (the latter two of which are shown here).

An alleged creature feeding or drinking beside a pond.
Photos by Ray Wallace.

Let's not mince words- this is, in all likelihood, a man in
a ridiculous costume posing next to a very dead, very
stuffed cougar. Photos by Ray Wallace.

Robert Michael Pyle writes of another in which the sasquatch is
shown tugging at an elk carcass. (Wallace says they kill these animals
with special round stones, hurling them like cannonballs, and
presented Pyle with one such stone he had collected as a gift.) I have
actually seen a few novices to the field take these pictures seriously,
but no one with any real amount of experience.

Why should he have gathered so much evidence over the years
when so many others search their whole lives and find nothing? "...I
have built roads where these giant-sized people have roamed for over
300 years," he wrote to Pyle, "and the only people sees B.F.s are

people like me that's running these big yellow Caterpillars as that's what the B.F.s are interested in as they will follow a cat around all day and watch us build roads." He added in conversation, "I've forgot more about Bigfoot than most people ever knew."

Wallace lives now in Toledo, Washington, reminding me of another old-timer from that city named Rant Mullens who once caused a minor stir by claiming he had actually created the entire Bigfoot phenomenon by accident back in 1924 by rolling some rocks down on some miners at Mt. St. Helens as a practical joke. The miners, he said, imagined it had been done by "giant hairy apes" and came up with the famous Ape Canyon story in which a group of enraged creatures attacked a cabin in retaliation for being shot at. Mullens really seemed to believe that every single one of the thousands of sightings and footprint reports since then (and even before, apparently) had somehow grown out of this. Wallace doesn't go nearly that far, but he has been accused by skeptics of much the same thing in that it's possible he may have faked much of the original evidence from northern California, though much of that evidence has stood up to scientific scrutiny and if the big-headed creatures in his films are the best he can do he just doesn't seem capable.

Veteran investigator John Green has said of Wallace that he is either "bats or having a hell of a good time," and one could interpret all his wild claims in either of these ways. It may very well be that when the Bluff Creek Bigfoot nearly put a stop to his road project in 1958, Ray Wallace vowed that he would have compensation one way or another. If so, he has been getting it ever since.

My favorite comment about Wallace is again from Robert Michael Pyle's "Where Bigfoot Walks: Crossing the Dark Divide." Pyle recounts the story of how he met a man who was devoting his life to finding Bigfoot, spending all his time and money in a seemingly fruitless attempt to capture greatness.

"I wanted to shake him and tell him to get a life, or a job. I did the next best thing: I told him to go see Ray Wallace. I wasn't sure if it was unkind, and if so, to which one?"

IVAN MARX

There is one more special case whose work is displayed in this section of the Gallery, a man about whom an entire book could easily be written. Indeed, not just one but two movies have been done about him and what he produced, and when it comes to claims of Bigfoot on film, he was far and away the most famous (or infamous) individual

next to Roger Patterson, and the most prolific by a long shot. But like Ray Wallace, none of his many films and photos are taken seriously by most investigators. Also, like Ray, he was most definitely an amusing down-home character who loved to sit in a comfortable chair and tell stories. But unlike Wallace, he seemed- for a time at least- to make a real effort to put his material forth and get it accepted, not just pulling it out now and then for entertainment purposes. He did this despite the fact that- once again like Ray Wallace- most of it looks utterly ridiculous.

It is almost a shame to have to showcase the work of Ivan Marx only to point out its many shortcomings, especially now, for Marx passed away on December 18th, 1999, at the age of 78. But as his wife of 43 years Peggy said (as noted in an obituary in Daniel Perez's Bigfoot Times in June 2000), Ivan "enjoyed life to the fullest" and "did pretty much what he wanted to do." As a pure character, he will be missed.

Marx first made a name for himself as a bear hunting guide and photographer and developed an excellent reputation, working for the Fish & Wildlife Service in Alaska for a time before moving to California in 1946. It was there that he first became involved in the search for sasquatch, being hired by Tom Slick's Pacific Northwest Expedition to see if hunting dogs could be made to track the creature. This yielded no results.

Most of the next decade passed without any major contributions to the field by Marx, but in 1969 an episode occurred that would become one of the most famous in the annals of cryptozoology. Strange, misshapen footprints had been found around the town of

Bossburg in northeast Washington; the left foot made a standard 17" track familiar to sasquatch followers, but the right appeared badly crippled, missing one toe and bent at a severe angle with two bulges along the outside edge showing where the bones inside had separated. A number of investigators were attracted to Bossburg and stayed for some time, hoping to turn up the creature responsible for the tracks, and Ivan Marx was among the first to arrive. On December 13th, he and Rene Dahinden were checking an area along the shore of Roosevelt Lake- reservoir for Grand Coolie Dam- where meat scraps had been left as bait, and Marx was the first to find a now legendary line of 1,089 of "Cripple- Foot's" tracks in the snow.

The hunt was on, and Bigfoot fever gripped the competing teams of hunters in the Bossburg area for the better part of the winter, but no more significant finds were made. The tracks have since been declared by anthropologist Dr. Grover Krantz to be completely consistent with the anatomy that one would expect to find in a foot of such great size, making a hoax extremely unlikely. Considering the body of photographic work that Marx would become best known for in following years, him being the first to lay eyes on these landmark tracks seems quite ironic.

It began in October of 1970. Marx was still living at Bossburg, still hoping to turn something up after most everyone else had given up. Dahinden, at least, kept in regular touch with him to keep tabs on the situation, and now and then Marx would report that he had found a new track or two or perhaps a handprint, just enough to keep him going. The thoughts and motivations that go through a man's head at such times can be very diverse indeed, living in the aftermath of a major discovery that, despite its impact, has failed to excite the powers that be. Waiting, waiting, waiting for something more. Something, anything...

We have already looked at how men like Paul Freeman may have acted at such times. Marx's way of handling the situation was eventually chronicled in the Colville Statesman-Examiner:

"On the night of October 6th, an unidentified person called the Marx home, leaving a vague message that either a car or a train had struck a large upright creature on the highway about seven miles north of Bossburg. Marx was away at the time, but when he received the message... he left immediately for the area with a hunting dog he hoped would follow the spoor of the Sasquatch, if indeed that was what it actually was.

"Marx was armed with nothing more than a Bolex 16mm movie camera with a 17mm lens, a 35mm Nikon, and a two-way radio with which he had contact with rancher Don Byington, who was in the area by the time Marx's dog had located the creature.

"The day was heavily overcast with smoke... when Marx jumped the creature in the bottom of a dense draw and began filming. The initial footage shows a large black upright figure moving stealthily but rapidly through the dense growth, but only in silhouette.

"Marx pressed the pursuit with his hound, forcing the Sasquatch into a clearing where, with his movie camera set at f 2.8, he took the remarkably clear footage of an impressive-looking creature.

"On the screen, the Sasquatch is shown moving from right to left at an angle of about forty-five degrees away from the photographer.

"Distance from the subject, according to Marx, ranged from twenty-five feet to more than a hundred feet as it made its way into the heavy underbrush on the far side of the clearing.

"Probably the most impressive part of the film, besides its extreme clarity, is the fact that the Sasquatch is visibly injured, holding its right arm tightly to its chest and using its long muscular left arm for compensating balance.

"Also, both ankles of the creature seem badly skinned, the wounds showing plainly raw against the black hair of the legs and feet.

"In watching the frames singly, the injured or skinned area appears to extend onto the bottom of one foot, and possibly on both feet, which would account for the apparent pain-filled movements of the frightened creature.

"As the Sasquatch is nearing the far side of the clearing, a twisted tree limb is stepped on, bouncing up and striking it above knee level. Marx, the following day, photographed this stick which was ten feet long. In comparison, the creature photographed would have stood about nine feet tall and Marx estimated its weight as that of two large bears, or around seven to eight hundred pounds.

"The only thing the film is lacking is facial features on the creature. Twice while crossing the clearing, the Sasquatch turned its head to glare at Marx. The first time it turned 180 degrees and uttered a weird scream which was heard by Byington, positioned on a ridge nearby. The second time it turned a full 360 degrees, appearing quite confused, but the lack of light prevented any facial features from showing plainly...

"Marx said he continued pursuit of the creature until darkness prevented further advance, and when the trail was recovered the following day, it led through a maze of rugged terrain and finally to a body of water where it was lost. He feels the Sasquatch is very old and apparently hurt quite badly."

Ivan Marx's famous Bossburg film. Often mentioned, seldom seen.

Very comical film by Marx of a creature cavorting in the snow.

Most sasquatch investigators were apparently led to believe that Marx's film was genuine. In retrospect, this seems rather amazing, since, in comparison to the Patterson film they were already well familiar with, it does not look real at all. The story that went with it is also puzzling in that a recent road accident seems to have been concocted as a reason for the creature's injuries when the tracks at Bossburg had already been appearing crippled for well over a year. Nevertheless, interest was high in the film, and a number of financial offers were made for it. Marx actually turned down a check for $25,000.

The offer he finally ended up taking came from Peter Byrne, who a few years later would be the founder of the Bigfoot Information Center in The Dalles, Oregon. Byrne agreed to pay Marx a monthly salary as a sasquatch hunter while the film stayed locked in a safe deposit box.

But a hoax under so much scrutiny is bound to unravel. Don Byington, the rancher Marx had been in contact with during the filming, had two young children who kept lingering in the background saying that they knew where the secret location of the filming was, and that it was on their father's property. In the spring of 1971, Byrne finally paid attention to them and was led to a spot he immediately recognized from the film. A branch the supposedly nine-foot creature had brushed its head against was found to be less than six feet above the ground. Further analysis of the site then revealed that Marx could not possibly have used the equipment he said he had used to shoot the film and that he had, in fact, used a telephoto lens, not a regular one. Finally, it was learned that Marx had been seen in Spokane not long before the filming buying several pieces of fur.

I met Peter Byme in October of 1989, at which time he described how Marx had "skipped town" in a hurry when he got wind that the game was up. When Byme went to confront him, he was long gone, and as a final insult, when he opened the safe deposit box, he found that he had not been given the real film but only a bunch of scrap.

The Bossburg film was shown in the David Wolper documentary "Monsters: Mysteries or Myths" hosted by "Twilight Zone" star Rod Serling (implying that it may be real), and one frame from it was featured on the t.v. show "In Search Of with Leonard Nimoy during a segment with Peter Byme (making it quite clear that it is not).

But Marx was far from finished. On October 21st, 1972 (timed to coincide with the fifth anniversary of the Patterson film, perhaps?), he appeared on the t.v. show "You Asked For It" with another film, this one shot in northern California and showing a creature in a snow-storm. Marx said he had tracked it for some distance and then been able to predict where it would appear and be waiting for it with his camera at the ready.

There is some confusion here, however. In "Sasquatch/Bigfoot: The Search for North America's Incredible Creature" by Don Hunter & Rene Dahinden, the "You Asked For It" film is said to show a white creature that looks completely ridiculous as it flops clumsily along through the snow. ("There was little doubt that what we were watching was a snowjob in a blizzard.") But in the movies that have been produced about Marx, there is a blizzard sequence that matches this description in most respects except that it shows a dark-haired creature. Whether the description of a white one was in error, or whether there are actually two different films involved here (in which case the "You Asked For It" film has been seen nowhere else), a primate expert asked for his opinion on the t.v. show said it best: "I think it's a man in a beast's suit." A no-brainer, that.

We begin now to see the look of what became the typical Ivan

Marx Bigfoot, identified by its extremely pointed head. It almost seems as if he must have viewed the sagittal crest on the bare skull of a gorilla and not realized that the spaces on either side of it are filled in with flesh in the living animal.

Now we arrive at the aforementioned movies about Marx's life, the first of which was called "The Legend of Bigfoot" and was shown widely in theaters in 1975. Though it is presented as a straight and serious documentary, this movie is rife with total fiction and even has someone else's voice dubbed over Marx's rather unsophisticated country drawl as he narrates the story. A whole host of photos and films appears, indicating that he must have been very busy indeed in the few years since Bossburg.

First, we see a series of seven goofy looking shots of the typical pointy-headed creature (including close-up facial views), along with a photo said to be taken in Alaska in April of 1973 that has been shown in a number of books of a dark creature sitting motionless on a flat rock in the middle of a sheer rocky cliff face, just as a man would sit in a chair. A big shaggy mane surrounds its head. Peter Byrne told me in 1989 that this was not a man in a costume but a mannequin of some kind. Here it is simply shown without comment, but in the December 1973 issue of Saga magazine, it was said to have been taken at a distance of 280 yards and displayed as "The most sensational Bigfoot picture ever taken."

Next comes the Bossburg story, or at least a version of it that has nothing whatsoever to do with reality. As Marx tells it, he had been hearing stories about Bigfoot for years as he went about his business as a hunting guide and photographer but never believed them until he began to see signs of the creature himself. (Fiction- He makes no mention of having been an employee of Tom Slicks's Pacific Northwest Expedition in search of Bigfoot in 1960.) Cautiously he began to pursue these signs, feeling foolish all the while, until he ran out of money. Then he took a job at Bossburg to film a cinnamon bear. (Fiction- It was Bigfoot he was there for.) "Then I saw it," he says in his narration, "a deformed version of the track I'd seen so often." (So, where was Rene Dahinden? Throughout the movie, Marx seems to make himself out as the only person in the country searching for the creature.) And when he saw the cripple-foot tracks, he says, the creature was right there, and he filmed it. The entire story of how he had responded to a call of a creature involved in an accident and the involvement of rancher Don Byington are nowhere to be found, and his comment about what happened next is laughable: "Scientists challenged my film, but it stood up under every conceivable test... experts who challenged my word but claimed credit for my film and profited by it on lecture circuits." None of that ever happened. Marx, character that he was, must be given credit for his vivid imagination.

Next, "The Legend of Bigfoot" moves to Alaska, where Marx did spend five years with the Fish & Wildlife Service. No mention of that is made, but there is a lot of native lore on the creature presented as Marx tries to determine migration routes from Alaska to the Pacific Northwest and predict where the creature might appear along the way. "If you wish to see the King of the Animals," a native tells him, "he breeds in the mating ground of the Alaskan moose." (It is also stated that the reason no dead bodies of Bigfoot are ever found is because they carry their dead up to Alaska and toss them into crevasses in the glaciers where they are ground to bits.) A creature is then spotted from the air by

Photo by Ivan Marx from Alaska in April, 1973 of a
creature sitting on a cliff face - later said to be a
mannequin of some kind.

A lovely riverbank scene. Two Ivan Marx films from
Alaska.

Creature alleged to be feeding at a place called Beaver Swamp. Two Ivan Marx films from Alaska.

Marx and a bush pilot, who land and film it. The film shows it at a considerable distance walking on a riverbank, actually a very beautiful daylight shot of the flowing river in the foreground and mountains in the back, but the creature is too far away to make out any detail.

Finally, Marx determines that he should be able to intercept the creatures in their migration at a place called Beaver Swamp, but where exactly this is is not made clear. He stakes it out and, sure enough, two creatures duly appear- one 7 feet tall and the other 5 1/2 feet, splashing in the water and feeding on swamp grass as he films them from his place of concealment. The parting shot is of a creature disappearing dramatically below the horizon, and I remember my first reaction being simply, "Oh, brother."

The other movie showcasing Marx's films is more of a true documentary in that it does not try to be some kind of slick, dramatic Hollywood production, appearing not in theaters but strictly on home video. "In the Shadow of Bigfoot" came out in 1983, featuring Marx's real voice this time as well as showing his wife Peggy and their home in Burney, California, where they lived surrounded by several animals, and presenting several more photos and films not seen in the previous movie. In fact, there is no crossover at all between the two, nothing from the first one in the second and vice-versa. A narrator gives some factual background on the sasquatch phenomenon in general, but again almost no mention is made of anyone besides Marx ever having investigated it in the Pacific Northwest.

Toward the beginning, a photo is shown without comment of a creature in silhouette sitting on a rock in what looks like meditation posture. (Bigfoot doing yoga?) During this segment, Marx talks about his upbringing and how his father taught him how to track and to live in the wilderness, and about Bigfoot, but later in the movie, he says he didn't believe in the creature until later in life.

Then comes one of the most well-known of the Ivan Marx stories next to Bossburg, the "shower scene" photos of Mt. Lassen, California, taken some time in the early 1980s. Marx says he was out of movie film at the time, so he was using a Nikon camera when he saw a creature standing in a marshy area and dousing itself with water to rid its body of mosquitoes. What is either meant to be prominent male genitalia or simply part of the costume sagging is visible in the photos. Whoever is in the suit this time is certainly going to a lot of effort to put on a good show.

Immediately following the shower scene is a series of six photos showing some typically vague-looking creatures in dense woods, shown without comment. These actually look like they could be the real thing were it not for their source.

The next thrilling tale from Marx's story involves the shooting of a creature that charged him and his wife as they were out trekking somewhere in northern California. Peggy is said to have shot the film as the familiar black, pointy-headed, human-proportioned creature ran towards them. A rifle shot is heard- fired by Marx- and the creature goes down, then rolls dramatically on the ground in pain for a moment before crawling back into the woods. But not to anger any animal rights proponents out there, it is made clear that the wounded creature recovers and makes a truly theatrical exit over the top of a ridge, turning for one last look toward the camera before disappearing.

The snowstorm film is also shown, and is said to have been shot during the making of the movie. This is totally at odds with the earlier date of the "You Asked For It" film (if they are in fact the same, which actually seems doubtful), but accurate dates mean very little in Marx's story.

You tell me - does Bigfoot practice yoga? Marx portrayed this creature in meditation posture.

The wounded creature limps into the woods. Two frames from Marx's "Shooting Incident" film.

As the creature looks back, we get one of the best views of the extremely pointed head often portrayed by Marx. Two frames from Marx's "Shooting Incident" film.

I need a bath! Marx's famous "Shower Scene" photos from Mt. Lassen.

Marx's famous "Shower Scene" photos from Mt. Lassen.

One of a series of six photos by Marx of creatures in the woods. These would actually look almost real if one did not know their source.

Here the film is said to have been taken from inside a snow igloo that Marx constructed to lay in wait for the creature, and he is shown getting into it. (So who was filming him?) Grunting sounds are heard as the ridiculous-looking beast shambles about through the snowy trees.

Curiously, "In the Shadow of Bigfoot" also leaves the west and travels to the east, exploring sasquatch sightings in both Florida and the New York-Vermont area. The Vermont photo covered earlier in this book is shown and is said to have been taken "just two months ago," which is, of course, inconsistent with its established date of 1976. In this segment, we hear from Prof. Warren Cook of Castleton State College in Vermont, an anthropologist specializing in Native American studies (now deceased). Amazingly, Cook endorsed all the Ivan Marx footage and seemed to think it was the most incredible thing he had ever seen, once appearing in an interview on CNN to promote the release of "In the Shadow of Bigfoot." He investigated sightings in his part of the country and was a rarity in being one of the few scientists who took the existence of sasquatch seriously, but it is sad to hear him embarrass himself by praising Marx's films and pointing out what looks to him to be realistic anatomical details in them. But then again, I suppose he was never truly shamed as long as he died still believing.

While Prof. Cook is talking, a very vague photo is shown of a creature peering out of the shadows of some woods, possibly holding something in its arms. Again there is no comment about it.

Another photo with no explanation behind it- showing a typical Marx creature bending at the waist- is flashed while a sasquatch witness named Judy Ramirez is describing her sighting. Ramirez is shown a slide of one of Marx's "shower scene" photos and says what she saw looked exactly like it.

Finally, there is a photo featured in the movie that seems to be credited to Marx, but which was previously shown in the May 11th, 1981, San Francisco Chronicle and said to have been taken by one Mr. C. Thomas Biscardi. It shows a black humanoid silhouette emerging from some trees, apparently approaching the camera with a determined step. The article in the Chronicle stated:

"A man who has been searching for Bigfoot for nearly a decade offered this photograph of the elusive man-ape yesterday. C. Thomas Biscardi of San Jose, president of Amazing Horizons, Inc., conceded that the front-view photo of a large ape-like figure emerging from a clump of trees may not be enough to convince skeptics. He said that his next step is to capture the creature.

"Biscardi, 32, claims to have seen Bigfoot on two occasions. He said his latest encounter occurred April 12th during a three-day expedition on Mount Lassen.

"'It was 10:45 a.m. when we saw it coming out of the thickets and trees. The creature we had been tracking for two days, was right there, about 100 yards from us. We were scared to death,' recounted Biscardi. 'It was a male, 7-foot-4, some 450 pounds.'"

Biscardi happens to be the Executive Director and Associate Producer of "In the Shadow of Bigfoot," and his company Amazing Horizons, Inc. is the movie's distributor. One must wonder if the "we" he refers to means himself and Ivan Marx, as he is also listed as having been the sponsor of the search that resulted in Marx's well-known cliff face photo from Alaska in 1973.

Another pointy-headed Ivan Marx creature, this one featured in "The Werewolf Book" by Brad Steiger.

However, his name is not attached to the previous movie, "The Legend of Bigfoot," in which that photo appeared. (It may be my imagination, but the Biscardi photo seems to resemble a frame from Marx's "shooting incident" film.)

So much for the movies of Marx's life. With completely fictional tellings of formerly true stories and dates that are as changeable as the weather, they are good for entertainment value only, and as a means to make one's Bigfoot video collection complete.

I will mention just one more picture from Marx's voluminous collection, appearing in 1999's "The Werewolf Book" by Brad Steiger (certainly a stretch, by any means). Said to be from a 1977 film, it shows yet another pointy-headed black creature walking along a northern California stream bank, tall but suspiciously slender for an animal commonly described as gigantic.

There are probably still some out there who believe in the Marx footage. After all, he did discover those famous cripple-foot tracks at Bossburg in 1969. He also produced plaster casts of some supposed sasquatch handprints that Dr. Grover Krantz has declared genuine (and I can neither support nor deny that). It is a maddening paradox, really, that he should have found it necessary to back up such significant finds with such blatantly outrageous films. Yet even a few of those films have been taken seriously.

In the 1975 book "The Mysterious Monsters" by Robert & Frances Gunette- a companion book to a movie of the same name- Marx's Alaska films are described in positive terms:

"In Alaska, in 1973, and again in 1975, Marx shot more film of the Bigfoot creatures. The first Alaskan film is a strikingly beautiful shot of a giant creature wading in a running stream. Shot from a long distance away, the creature's features are not distinguishable. But it is large, and covered with dark hair. The creature is seen moving out of frame, apparently having heard a sound. The second and most recent film shows the creature feeding by another stream, eating what Ivan described to me as 'moose moss.'" (The "Beaver Swamp" film.)

The same book calls the "You Asked For It" footage "an astonishing piece of film."

But another book- John Green's 1978 comprehensive study "Sasquatch: The Apes Among Us"- gave us what will probably always be the most enduring essay on Ivan Marx. In a reverent little chapter entitled simply "Ivan," Green recounts many amusing tales from his association with him, including Marx's method of catching cougars by the tail. "For all, I know about catching cougars," Green writes, "maybe that's how you do it, but I don't intend to try it, and I don't suggest it to anyone else either." The chapter was basically the comic relief in an otherwise very scholarly book, but not at all in an insulting way. In reading it, one can easily feel the affection for this colorful

character despite all his attempts to fool the experts and the public. He was, at the end of it all, a true outdoorsman, and he definitely made his mark.

After Ivan's death, his wife Peggy wrote to Bigfooter Daniel Perez, "Think he'd like to be remembered for his work with bears."

Sounds good to me.

Credited to both Ivan Marx and his partner C. Thomas
Biscardi, this photo was supposed to show a
sasquatch emerging from the woods on Mt. Lassen.

5

IN CONCLUSION

I would like to make a prediction, if I may, of the type of review this book is likely to get within the sasquatch community when it appears:

"'Big Footage' provides next to nothing in the way of hard evidence for the existence of the creatures it claims to showcase, being instead, a loosely assembled collection of photographic cases that have in many instances been long since cast aside as useless by serious investigators. What is the point?"

I know, folks, I know. I fully realize and accept that several of the more vocal and opinionated members of the field will miss the point of this book entirely. There are many out there who, when confronted with a dubious or definitely fake photo or film, will do all they can to bury it under a deluge of scholarly criticism and do all but erase it from the face of the Earth. To even discuss the films of Ivan Marx or Paul Freeman, for example, is looked on by these people as an exercise in futility, and I have often been met with a surprisingly venomous reaction to such discussion.

What's the point? How can this help to prove that sasquatch really exists?

But there is an interesting parallel here. These same vociferous investigators are often embroiled in personality clashes and feuds of all kinds within the field, battling each other rather than battling the elements in a real concrete search for the creature- or evidence thereof- that has so impassioned their lives.

So again- what's the point? How can this help to prove that sasquatch really

exists?

I know sasquatch exists, for I have seen one. My sighting was fleeting, but with the evidence, I have seen since that time, I have long since outlived any need for it to have occurred to convince me. But I have devoted other books to that end. The point of the volume you hold in your hands now is anecdotal, not scientific, and it drives home the fact that few in the sasquatch field seem to have noticed over the years. That is that the number of individual photos and films claimed to show sasquatches or similar creatures over the years- from the early 20th century until today- is over 100. How does this compare to the number of UFO or ghost photos? It is competitive, certainly. And what percentage of the total can be considered or at least suspected as being genuine? It will probably never be known for sure, but the numbers are probably about equal in all of these fields.

Several of the examples in this collection are outright frauds, and that is undeniable. But these must not be ignored, for a day will come when the sasquatch is proven beyond doubt to exist in the concrete world of zoology, and at that point, comparison to the fakes will make the genuine articles stand out all the more as important evidence, perhaps even as clues to the animals' behavior in the wild. Against all odds, pitted against an onslaught of tabloid-minded hoaxes, the real photographic evidence for sasquatch will survive to help flesh out the necessarily vague impressions that will exemplify this creature's entry into a scientific reality.

Roger Patterson did film a real live sasquatch in 1967. Many, many others claim to have done the same. Doesn't the law of averages state that at least some of them are likely to be right?

Many, however, are either simply wrong or outrightly lying. But we can not deny that even those people are a part of the whole sasquatch phenomenon- a phenomenon that is at once scientific, cultural, and psychological. To that end, at least, all these cases have their own special value.

6

APPENDIX

ALL KNOWN FILM CLAIMS

- Near Lilooet, British Columbia - Early 20th century (photo).
- Alaska - 1948 (film).
- Ray Wallace, Northern California and other locations - 1958 and other dates (films and photos).
- Zack Hamilton, 3 Sisters Wilderness, Oregon- 1960 (photos).
- Lennart Strand & Alden Hoover, near Sonora, California- February 28, 1963 (photo).
- Leroy Yarborough & Jerry Oakes, near Caddo, Texas- Summer, 1964 (film).
- Dave Churchill, near The Dalles, Oregon- June, 1967 (photos).
- Roger Patterson & Robert Gimlin, Bluff Creek, California- October 20, 1967 (film).
- Near Nelagony, Oklahoma- 1967 (photo).

- Robert James, Jr. & Leroy Larwick, near Sonora, California- January 6, 1968 (photo).
- Allen Plaster, Lake Worth outside Fort Worth, Texas- Summer or Fall, 1969 (photo).
- Ron Smith, Cub Lake near Darrington, Washington - Summer, 1970 (photo).
- Ivan Marx, near Bossburg, Washington- October 7, 1970 (film).
- Ivan Marx, Northern California- Winter, early 1972 (?) (film).
- Waterfall Forks, Washington- 1972 (photo).
- Idaho- 1972 (photo).
- Mrs. B.S., near Houston, British Columbia- 1972 (film).
- Mr. B.S., near Houston, British Columbia- 1972 (photo).
- Ivan Marx, Alaska- April, 1973 (photo).
- Ivan Marx, Alaska- 1973 (film).
- Rosemary Tobash, Kootenay National Park, British Columbia- 1974 (photo).
- North Park, Allegheny County, Pennsylvania- March 28, 1975 (photos).
- Joe Speck, Samuel P. Taylor State Park, California- August, 1975 (film).
- J.W., near Orofino, Idaho- October 24, 1975 (film).
- John Sohl, Citrus County, Florida- November, 1975 (photo).
- Harewood Park, Maryland- November, 1975 (photo).
- Ivan Marx, "Beaver Swamp," Alaska- 1975 (film).
- Barbara Pretula, East Kootenay-Kimberly area, British Columbia- September, 1976 (photo).
- Near Chittenden, Vermont- October, 1976 (photo).
- Near Ennis, Montana- October, 1976 (photos).
- Near Ruthven, Ontario- June 4, 1977 (photos).
- Silver Lake, California- August, 1977 (photos).
- Karl Blagge, Near Ukiah, California- September, 1977 (photos).
- Mr. & Mrs. Frank White, Mt. Baker claimed but actually

Lummi Indian Reservation, Washington- October 7, 1977 (film).

- Near Tupelo, Mississippi- Fall, 1977 (film).
- Dart (?), Little Eagle, Standing Rock Reservation, South Dakota- late 1977 (photos).
- Ivan Marx, Northern California - 1977 (film).
- Near Westfield, Massachusetts- September 10, 1978 (photos).
- Bigfoot Lake, Washington - 1978 (photo).
- Washington - 1978 (film, but likely a confusion with #34).
- Marion Schubert, California- 1978 (photo).
- Mt. Rainier, Washington - 1979 (photos).
- Near Index or Monte Cristo, Washington- 1979 (photo).
- South-Central Canada, possibly Boundary Waters Canoe Area- late 1970s (photo).
- Ivan Marx, Mt. Lassen, California- early 1980s (photos).
- Lyle Vann, Southern California- October 21, 1980 (photo).
- Lyle Vann, Angeles National Forest, California- January 6, 1981 (photo).
- C. Thomas Biscardi, Mt. Lassen, California- April 12, 1981 (photo).
- Near Beacon Rock, Washington- 1982 (photos).
- Bubba Williamson, Green Swamp near Aubumdale, Florida- March, 1984 (photo).
- Anthony B. Wooldridge, Northern India- March 6, 1986 (photos).
- Lyle Vann, Northern Arizona- Spring, 1987 (photo).
- Paul Freeman, Blue Mountains near Walla Walla, Washington- 1987 (photos).
- Near McCarthur, Ohio- May, 1988 (film).
- Derry Township, Pennsylvania- June 29, 1988 (photos).
- Scape Ore Swamp near Bishopville, South Carolina- Summer, 1988 (photo).
- Duane & Paul Freeman, Blue Mountains near Walla Walla, Washington- October 5, 1988 (photos).

- Betty Parks & Richard Myers, Coshocton County, Ohio- November 1, 1988 (photo).
- Patapsco Valley State Park near Baltimore, Maryland- 1988 (various videos).
- Lyle Vann, Northern Arizona- April 17, 1989 (photos).
- Don Keating & Richard Mortz, Coshocton County, Ohio- September 15,
- (video).
- Jack Rowley, Asian Republic of Kirgizia- September, 1991 (photo).
- Don Keating, Coshocton County, Ohio- December 22, 1991 (video).
- Mt. Rainier, Washington- 1991 (photo).
- Coshocton County, Ohio (?) - early 1991 (?) (video).
- Paul Freeman, Blue Mountains near Walla Walla, Washington- April 14, 1992 (video).
- Robert Daigle, Ohio- Summer, 1992 (various videos).
- Robert Daigle, Ohio - June 6, 1992 (video).
- Don Keating, Ohio - August 2, 1992 (video).
- Paul Freeman, Blue Mountains near Walla Walla, Washington- August 20,
- (video).
- Daryl Owen & Scott Herriott, Klamath area, California- October 12, 1991 (videos).
- North Cascades, Washington- 1992 (photo).
- Eastern Washington (?)- early 1993 (?) (video).
- Steven Williams, near Molalla, Oregon- July 27, 1993 (photo).
- Oregon- Fall, 1993 (photos).
- Location unknown - 1993 (photo).
- D.S., Devils Lake State Park north of Madison, Wisconsin- 1st week of January, 1994 (photo).
- Sharon Jones, near Molalla, Oregon- January, 1994 (photos).

- Wild Creek, Mt. Baker/Snoqualmie National Forest, Washington- July 11, 1995 (photos).
- Craig Miller, Colin & Anna-Marie Goddard, Jedediah Smith Redwoods State Park near Crescent City, California- August 28, 1995 (video).
- Near Coon Rapids, Minnesota - Summer or Fall, 1995 (video, but very doubtful this actually exists).
- Danny Sweeten, Sam Houston National Forest, San Jacinto County, Texas- October 5, 1995 (video).
- Southern Alaska- January, 1997 (video).
- Julie Ellif & Wayne Oliver, Chilliwack/Agassiz, British Columbia area- May 5 or 6, 1997 (video).
- David Shealy, Florida Everglades- November, 1997 (photos).
- Vince Doerr, Ochopee, Florida - 1997 (photo).
- Mary Green (?), Tennessee - February, 1998 (photo).
- Chad W. Michael, location unknown- November 24, 1998 (video).
- Jim Smith/anonymous Internet user, Lakeport, Florida- March 20, 2000 (web cam shot).
- David Shealy, Florida Everglades - July 8, 2000 (video).
- Near Breckenridge Mountain, California- September 4, 2000 (video).
- Steve Piper, Brindabella ranges, Australia- September 8, 2000 (video).

DATES UNKNOWN

- Peggy Marx & Ivan Marx, Northern California (film).
- Charles Edson, Fremont, California area (?) (various films and photos).
- Jon Eric Beckjord, California Sierras (various photos).
- East Liberty, Ohio (photo).

- Himalayas claimed, but actually Mammoth Mountain, California (video).
- Ohio (photos).
- R. Ravzhir, Mongolia (photo).
- 99-103. Locations unknown (four photos and one film or video).
- (Obviously fictional tabloid pictures not featured.)
- With the multiple films and photos of Charles Edson, Jon Eric Beckjord, Ray Wallace, Lyle Vann, and Ivan Marx the real number of claims is actually far in excess of 100.

7

BIBLIOGRAPHY

Information in this book has come from a wide range of sources, including personal correspondence, word of mouth, and just my own memory. The following listing is as complete as possible, but unfortunately, some items such as individual news clippings have been lost over time.

BOOKS

- Bartholemew, Paul & Bob; William Brann and Bruce Hallenbeck. "Monsters of the Northwoods." Utica, NY: North Country Books, 1992.
- Bayanov, Dmitri. "America's Bigfoot: Fact, Not Fiction." Moscow: CryptoLogos Books, 1996.
- Bord, Janet & Colin. "The Bigfoot Casebook." Harrisburg, PA: Stackpole Books, 1982.
- Bord, Janet & Colin. "The Evidence for Bigfoot and Other Man-Beasts." New York: Sterling Publications, 1984.
- Byrne, Peter. "The Search for Big Foot: Monster, Myth or Man?" Washington: Acropolis Books Ltd., 1975.

- Crook, Cliff. "The Abominable Snowjob." Bothell, WA: Privately published.
- Gaffron, Norma. "Bigfoot: Opposing Viewpoints." San Diego, CA: Greenhaven Press, 1989.
- Green, John. "On the Track of the Sasquatch." Agassiz, B.C.: Cheam Publishing Ltd., 1968.
- Green, John. "On the Track of the Sasquatch- 1980s Edition." Victoria, B.C.: Cheam Publishing Ltd., 1980.
- Green, John. "The Sasquatch File." Agassiz, B.C.: Cheam Publishing Ltd., 1970.
- Green, John. "Sasquatch: The Apes Among Us." Seattle: Hanover House, 1978.
- Guenette, Robert & Frances. "The Mysterious Monsters." Los Angeles: Sun Classic Pictures, 1975.
- Hall, Mark A. "The Yeti, Bigfoot & True Giants." Minneapolis: Mark A. Hall Publications, 1997.
- Howe, Linda Moulton. "Glimpses of Other Realities Vol. 2- High Strangeness." New Orleans, LA: Paper Chase Press, 1998.
- Hunter, Don with Rene Dahinden. "Sasquatch/Bigfoot: The Search for North America's Incredible Creature." Buffalo, NY: Firefly Books, 1993.
- Keating, Don. "The Buckeye Bigfoot." Newcomerstown, OH: Privately published, 1993.
- Krantz, Grover. "Big Footprints: A Scientific Inquiry into the Reality of Sasquatch." Boulder, CO: Johnson Books, 1992.
- McDougal, Dennis. "The Yosemite Murders." New York: Ballantine Publishing Group, 2000.
- Miller, Marc E.W. "The Legends Continue- Adventures in Cryptozoology." Kempton, IL: Adventures Unlimited Press/Publishers Network, 1998.
- Napier, John. "Bigfoot: The Yeti and Sasquatch in Myth and Reality." New York: E.P. Dutton, 1973.
- Orchard, Vance. "Bigfoot of the Blues." Walla Walla, WA:

Privately published, 1993.

- Patterson, Roger. "Do Abominable Snowmen of America Really Exist?" Yakima, WA: Franklin Press, 1966.
- Perez, Danny. "Bigfoot at Bluff Creek." Santa Cruz, NM: Danny Perez Publications, 1994.
- Pyle, Robert Michael. "Where Bigfoot Walks: Crossing the Dark Divide." New York: Houghton Mifflin Company, 1995.
- Smith, Carlton. "Murder at Yosemite." New York: St. Martin's Press, 1999.
- Steenburg, Thomas. "In Search of Giants: Bigfoot Sasquatch Encounters." Surrey, B.C. and Blaine, WA: Hancock House Publishers, 2000.
- Steiger, Brad. "The Werewolf Book." Farmington Hills, MI: Visible Ink Press, 1999.
- Time/Life "Mysteries of the Unknown" series. "Mysterious Creatures." Richmond, VA: Time/Life Books, 1988.
- Wasson, Barbara. "Sasquatch Apparitions." Bend, OR: Privately published, 1979.

NEWSLETTERS

- Cameron, Connie editor. The Bigfoot Co-Op- April 1989, June 1990, April 1993, October 1993, February 1994, June 1994, October 1996, February 1997, February 1998, April 1998, February 1999, August 2000.
- Crowe, Ray editor. The Track Record- #20- August 1992, #32- October 1993.
- Francis, Mark editor. North American Bigfoot Information Network Journal- #5- Winter/Spring 1992, #6- Summer/Fall 1992.
- Green, Bill editor. The Bigfoot Record- #2, #7, #16.
- Greenwell, J. Richard editor. "First Yeti Photos Spark Renewed Interest." The ISC Newsletter- Vol. 5, #4, Winter 1986.

- Perez, Daniel editor. <u>The Bigfoot Times</u>- December 1998, January 1999, January 2000, February 2000, March 2000, June 2000, July 2000, August 2000, September/October, 2000.
- Quast, Mike and Tim Olson, editors. <u>The Sasquatch Report</u>- #4- July 1990, #66- September 1995.
- Steiner, Ted and David Warner, editors. <u>Minnesota Bigfoot News</u>- September, 1978.

NEWSPAPERS

- Cleveland, OH <u>Plain Dealer</u>- January 9, 1989.
- <u>The Columbian</u>. December 15, 1995.
- Coshocton, OH <u>Tribune</u>. February 1992.
- "Is This the Dread Man-Animal?" <u>San Francisco Chronicle</u>. December 14, 1965. Latrobe, PA <u>Bulletin</u>. July 14, 1988.
- <u>Mainichi Daily News</u>. March 20, 1988.
- "The Monster Returns- Local Fliers Capture Creature on Film." Sonora, CA <u>Union-Democrat</u>, January 8, 1968.
- "2 Prominent Bigfoot Believers no Longer Toeing the Line." <u>USA Today</u>, January 11, 1999.
- <u>San Francisco Chronicle</u>. May 11, 1981.
- <u>Springfield Republican</u>, February 11, 1979.
- Striker, Denny. "Bigfoot Seen, Photographed." Colville, WA Statesman <u>Examiner</u>, November 13, 1970.
- Walla Walla, WA <u>Union-Bulletin</u>, October 7, 1988.

OTHER PERIODICALS

- <u>BBC Wildlife</u>. September 1986.
- Dart, Sam. "A Bigfoot Sighting in South Dakota." <u>Argosy</u>, March, 1978.
- <u>Fate</u>, July 1963.

- Idaho State Journal, November 28, 1995.
- Idaho State University News & Notes. December 11, 1995.
- Saga, December 1973.
- Sanderson, Ivan T. "First Photos of 'Bigfoot,' California's 'Abominable Snowman.'" Argosy, February 1968.

MOVIES

- "Big Foot: Man or Beast. A Rainbow Adventure... A Film Report." American National Enterprises.
- "The Blair Witch Project." Haxan Films/Artisan Entertainment, Daniel Myrick and Eduardo Sanchez directors, 1999.
- "The Ghost and the Darkness." Constellation Films/Paramount Pictures, Michael Douglas and Steven Reuther producers, 1996.
- "In the Shadow of Bigfoot." Amazing Horizons, Inc., C. Thomas Biscardi producer, 1983.
- "The Legend of Bigfoot." World Pictures, Stephen Houston Smith producer, 1975.
- "Monsters: Mysteries or Myths." Smithsonian Institution, David Wolper producer, 1974.
- "The Mysterious Monsters." Schick Sun Classic Pictures, Inc., David Wolper producer, 1975.

TELEVISION

- "Ancient Mysteries- Bigfoot." A & E, 1994.
- "Hard Copy- The New Bigfoot Video." Paramount Pictures Television Group, October 29, 1992.
- "Hard Copy- The Playmate and the Primate." Paramount Pictures Television Group, 1995.
- "In Search Of- Bigfoot." Leonard Nimoy host, 1977.
- The Learning Channel, February 28, 2000.

- "Paranormal Borderline." UPN-Paramount Pictures Television Group. "Sightings." Tim White host, FOX, 1992.
- "Strange Universe." Danny Sweeten featured, Chris-Craft/United Television, Rysher Entertainment.
- "Those Incredible Animals." Loretta Swit host, Discovery.
- "The Tonight Show with Jay Leno." Anna-Marie Goddard guest, NBC, 1995. WBAP (Fort Worth, TX) news broadcast, August 4, 1964.
- "World's Greatest Hoaxes- Secrets Finally Revealed." Lance Henriksen host, FOX, December 28, 1998.
- "You Asked For It." Sandy Frank, October 21, 1972.

PERSONAL CORRESPONDENCES

- Jon Eric Beckjord, Malibu, CA
- Peter Byrne, Mt. Hood, OR
- Robert Daigle, Warren, MI
- Stan Gordon, Ligonier, PA
- John Green, Harrison Hot Springs, B.C.
- Joe Heinan, Moorhead, MN
- Joan Jeffers, Bradford, PA
- Don Keating, Newcomerstown, OH
- Wayne King, Caro, MI
- Tim Olson, Arcata, CA
- Mark Opsasnick, Riverdale, MD
- Daniel Perez, Norwalk, CA

ABOUT THE AUTHOR

 Mike Quast has been investigating reports of sasquatch in his home state of Minnesota since 1987, his interest piqued by his own sighting in 1976 at the age of eight. A resident of the city of Moorhead, he is the author of three previous books - "The Sasquatch in Minnesota" (1990), "Creatures of the North: The New Minnesota Sasquatch Encounters" (1991), and "The Sasquatch in Minnesota: Revised Edition" (1996). He was also the originator of the Sasquatch Report newsletter that ran from April, 1990 to January, 1997.

A graduate in commercial art from Northwest Technical College, Mike was struck with the high number of cases in which people across the country claimed to have captured the sasquatch on film and how most of them seemed to have gone largely unrecognized. Here he puts his artistic talents to use in depicting many of these pictures and describing the interesting stories that go with them.

CPSIA information can be obtained
at www.ICGtesting.com
Printed in the USA
LVHW020707221021
701184LV00020B/1384